Defending the Barrel & the Blade

Weapons Defenses of the
United States Krav Maga Association

MARK SLANE

"The wicked flee when no man pursues but the righteous are bold as a lion."
—Deut. 28:1

"Krav Maga, so that one may walk in peace."
—Imi Lichtenfeld

Dedicated to USKMA black belts; Matt Kissel, John Lovins, Brannon Hicks, John Burton, Scott Howard, Jason Holt, Sue Burton, Terri Rosen, Aaron Jannetti, Juan Acosta, Alexis Acosta, Russ Sweeney, Will Schneider, Jesse Tucker, David Inman, Brock Inman, Travis Dilman, Celia Webb, Ken Koepke, Ron Mendes, Jenna Herder, Dom Stouder, Danny Caudil, Fatimah Sayaad, Andrea Tabei, Heather Sutton, Dave Sutton, Ken Rundell, Karissa Trimpe, Shelley Campbell, Sean McVeigh, Terry Ryan, Jason Jannetti, Mike Walter, Danny Brandt, Darrell Walton, Micah Scott, Scott King, Dave Colina and Jared Ricart.

Also dedicated to the loves of my life; Tina, Crystal, Jewel, Taeson, Shae and my mama Diane.

Thanks to my "attackers" in the pictures of this book; Matt Kissell, Gabe Cohen, Danny Caudill, Taeson Slane and Jewel Slane.

A special thanks to SGT Brannon Hicks, the USKMA's co-lead instructor, for his countless hours in training perfecting these techniques.

Last but not least, a big thanks to Rory Miller for writing the forward to this book. Almost everything I know about real world violence and what has a chance of working against it comes from his writings. It is truly like writing a book on quarterbacking and having Peyton Manning write the forward for it...or a book about basketball and having Lebron write the forward. Thanks, my friend.

"The only defense against violent, evil people are good people who are more skilled at violence."
—SGT Rory Miller

My name is Mark Slane. I have been teaching martial arts and self defense (they are often not the same thing) since 1986. I am a fourth degree black belt in Taekwondo, a national tkd sparring champion (Lt. wt. 33-40 age group) and a third degree black belt in Krav Maga. I have written three self defense books (four counting this one), have had an article published in Black Belt Magazine, have trained with an Olympic gold medal winning boxer (Jerry Page), have coached dozens of national taekwondo medalists and champions, have taught thousands of citizens and hundreds of law enforcement officers Krav Maga and am the president and co-lead instructor (along with SGT Brannon Hicks) of the United States Krav Maga Association. Guess what? All of that means squat in the real world. Any punk with a weapon could end my life before I even realize that they are there. If faced with a knife wielding thug (or several knife wielding thugs) I would trade all of those credentials and all of that training for a ball bat (or, of course, a good handgun)! What I am saying here, and throughout this book, is that most self defense and martial arts gurus are teaching self defense techniques, not self defense! There is a big difference. It is not what you are learning (you can protect yourself with any art) that is important. IF you are attacked those techniques will degrade massively, to the point of being fairly worthless. What will save you is a go forward with hatred, rage and aggression mind set. As SGT Rory Miller says "the first person to go balls to the wall almost always wins".

Hollywood and self proclaimed "Masters" have blown so much smoke up our butts that we think there are magic techniques. We think certain arts will make us unbeatable. We think we can become unbeatable if we just find the perfect system to study. What will make us safe is the right mind set, studying what real violence is, realizing what the adrenalin (and other chemicals) dump will do to us under stress and perfecting the tool of violence. Good self defense training is about developing a switch to instantaneously go from overwhelmed, uncomprehending and terrified to going forward with rage, aggression and hatred to do the maximum amount of damage in the minimum amount of time...and then getting the heck out of there.

I have always loved Krav Maga's weapon's defenses. I have practiced these more than anything else in Krav. It intrigued me that, after watching the BS that TV and movies taught about weapons for so many years, if anyone had a handgun or shotgun close enough for me to touch, I am relatively safe. There is so much BS out there that people actually believe about weapons. Krav's stick, handgun and long gun defenses are amazing! I truly think I can teach anyone to take these away from a thug. Notice that I didn't say anything about a knife? Those are scary! Your best bet, if you can't run or access a ball bat is to just attack the attacker. Swing for the fences doing major damage as you try to block the thing.

Weapon disarms are a bit more technical then most everything else in Krav. Being choked, hit, hair grabbed, bear hugged, etc. is basically going off like a bomb and beating the crap out of whoever is trying to hurt you. With the weapon involved we can't just start swinging for the fences...we have to redirect or block the thing first.

All of these techniques in this book are the exact same we teach to law enforcement officers and military personnel. We take this job seriously! We have tweaked and changed these techniques over the years to make sure we are teaching the most battle tested, up to date, effective and best possible. Train hard, train often, train realistic attacks & scenarios and BE SAFE!!

History and Introduction

Imi Lichtenfeld is the founder of Krav Maga. Imi was a stud in his day. He was an all-European wrestler, boxer and gymnast. His dad was a well renowned police chief who was known for bringing in the hardened criminals that nobody else could. He was known equally well for the self-defense techniques that he taught his officers which were very advanced for the time. A young Imi worked with his dad closely on these techniques. Imi was also a Jew on the wrong side of the tracks right before the start of WWII. Imi was a legendary character. He and a few friends protected their barrio from gangs of Nazi youth quite often. Imi was also a very analytical man. He would usually win his fights but afterwards he would think "what if there were four more of them" or "what if they had sticks or knives." He quickly found out that the street was different from the ring. For example, his wrestling did no good on the street

as he saw that he couldn't be on the ground with one thug while the thug's friends were standing over him attempting to kick him in the head. Imi thankfully got out of Czechoslovakia before the war actually started. When Israel became a nation in 1948 Imi was so highly thought of that he was one of the men put in charge of the Israeli Defense Forces' hand to hand combat. One of the challenges that Imi faced in this role that are relevant for us today are that he had, in the IDF, both men and women. Therefore, he had to teach techniques that didn't rely on brute strength or size. Other challenges are that he had everyone in the country between the ages 18-55. He didn't have just the athletes but the ones who were completely unathletic and uncoordinated as well. This is why you will see no jump, spin, flying anything in Krav Maga. Krav Maga is simple, gross motor movements that anyone can do. He also had recruits for only six weeks in boot camp to train them. Whatever he taught had to be easy to learn and easy to remember. If you know anything about Israel's history you know that whatever was taught had to be effective as well. Krav Maga isn't a Martial Art where things are done because of tradition. Israelis don't care about tradition, they care about survival. If a technique comes along that is easier to learn or more effective they'll jump to that technique in a heartbeat. Krav Maga is probably the most battle tested hand to hand defense system in the world. Krav Maga has been used by the Israeli Defense Forces for many years. The IDF has a well earned reputation for using techniques that work in the real world. These techniques have been adopted by many law enforcement agencies across the United States. Techniques that are easy to learn, easy to remember under stress and, most importantly, extremely effective make Krav Maga the standard for Law Enforcement and Military defensive tactics.

Contents

Forward

by Rory Miller. Author of Mediations on Violence, Facing Violence, Force Decisions, Conflict Communication and several others

You know that sinking feeling you get when a friend says, "Hey, buddy, will you write a foreword for my book? It's on weapon disarms."

I dodged. I hedged. What I actually said was:

Basically, if these three things are in the book, I'm happy to do a foreword:

1) *Most gun disarms are based, subconsciously, on a threat who doesn't want to kill you in the first place (otherwise he would already have pulled the trigger) who is standing at a specific distance (gun in reach) and doesn't know how to hold it (all trained people and even most criminals go to retention position at that range). As such, the body mechanics (answer) is simple, but the <u>problem</u> most train for is fantasy.*

2) *Most blade attacks are assassinations, very close up and with the non-weapon hand used to control either the arm or the head.*

3) *Most likely scenario where a disarm (or escape) is appropriate includes being intimidated to a secondary crime scene which will likely involve a much smaller victim, a casual-looking grip (over the shoulder or upper arm) and the weapon concealed by the bodies of threat and victim. Lots of psychology, social stuff and tactics in this scenario.*

Mark chuckled, I'm sure, and sent me a few sample chapters. So here I am.

Mark Slane is a Krav guy, blood and bone. Dedicated, even fanatic. When I know nothing about a style, fanatics are the ones I like to learn from. Will I agree with everything they do? Of course not, but they will show you the best of their system.

For a Krav Maga practitioner, especially within USKMA, this is a textbook of techniques. As an outsider, this is an intro to the Krav attitude and the Krav method. Insider or outsider, there is something here for you.

This is a book of techniques, though Mark says repeatedly that technique is, at most, 40% of defense. There are lots of techniques in here, lots of detail, lots of stuff… none of which are primary for survival. As Mark says, "…it is all heart that gets them through it and heart on the street is worth more than any technique or system."

But heart is hard as hell to put in a book. So practice the techniques. Play with them. Experiment with different body sizes and strengths. See what works for you, at least mechanically. But remember that the mechanics are the least important part. Find a good instructor and good partners that can push your limits, comrades that will drive you to and beyond exhaustion. People that can find your freeze points and help you past them. People who can give you a taste of the fear and desperation that will always underlie these techniques.

As Mark says, "We survive with heart." The rest is details.

Rory Miller, Boston, Sept. 2014

Philosophy of Krav Maga

"Violence of motion trumps technique"
—Deputy US Marshall J. Jones

Forget techniques! Techniques are going to deteriorate massively when done under the stress, exhaustion and the adrenaline dump of a real world violent attack, it's guaranteed! Why do we insist on spending all of our training time perfecting techniques when that last statement is a truth that nobody can argue? .Ask any cop whom they would rather face A) a very proficient black belt martial artist or B) some nutso who wants to rip off their face and chew on their eyes. I have yet talked to one who didn't choose the martial artist!

If faced with a knife wielding maniac I would take a ball bat and an attitude over a black belt in any system, including krav maga! Aggression, rage and swinging with bad intentions would keep me safer than anything else I could do. The first person to go balls to the wall in a fight usually wins! Let's quit worrying about technique and work on becoming a fighter! A swinging for the fences, going forward, aggressive, full of hate and rage fighter! That's someone who will survive!

The main principle of Krav Maga that all others branch off of is STAY SAFE. We stay safe by first and foremost, not being there. Don't go to stupid places with stupid people to do stupid things! The second rule is RUN. Really, run when in danger…run when in doubt. I don't care if the local paper has a picture of me running from a knife wielding punk with the headline "Krav Maga expert runs from knife". I would be a smart, still living Krav Maga expert! Our third rule is to pick up something to whack the bad guy with. Why go into a knife with just my hands when I can pick up a pipe or stick and have distance and impact on my side? The fourth rule is to DESTROY the attacker. We aren't safe if we merely fend off the attacker but still have to go to an ER afterwards. We aren't safe if we win the fight but have months of rehab ahead of us. We are safe if we are unscathed. If we go hard, go first and go until the threat is gone we have a much better chance of being unscathed. Notice how far down the list that the actual Krav Maga techniques are used. If you get to the techniques you probably weren't paying attention or were in a stupid place to begin with!

Wikipedia says the principles of Krav Maga are: 1. Do as much damage in as little time as possible. 2. Change from defending to attacking as quickly as possible (including simultaneously). 3. Use items around you as weapons. 4. Be aware of everything that is happening around you. Let's look at these one at a time and think about why they make so much sense for self defense.

1) Do as much damage in as little time as possible. This is why we preach not to spar but to end things. Sparring is moving around, throwing a combo, backing out, changing levels, going back in, etc. This is never a good idea as it extends the time that we are in danger. The attacker may be a better sparer than we are and (more importantly) extending the fight gives his buddies time to get to you. As a wise man once said "every asshole has an asshole friend nearby". Our goal in a real world violence situation should be to end things and get out of there…as quickly as possible. This is why we teach to go forward with rage, swing as hard as you can and strike targets that do the most damage. Keep hitting until you can escape, which is when the attacker is unconscious generally.

2) Change from defending to attacking as quickly possible (including simultaneously). I talk about this in my self defense for women book. When we are attacked we are a victim. As soon as we fight back there is no longer a victim and an attacker, there are two opponents. Most scum bags are looking for a victim, not for someone who will fight back…and fight back hard!

3) Use items around you as weapons. Absolutely! I know some "great" unarmed knife defenses but why would I want to use them if there is a pipe laying close by? Something with impact and distance is a good idea…I bleed! A person with a weapon and just a small amount of training will beat a well trained person who is empty handed more often than not.

4) Be aware of everything that is happening around you. This is talking about self protection and being aware at all times. Self defense is you grabbed me so I had to react. Self protection is I saw you coming and avoided you. Self defense is I went into a seedy looking bar and, sure enough, I got into a fight. Self protection is the bar looked seedy so I didn't go in. Self defense is you were hitting me so I smacked you back. Self protection is you were in my space looking like a threat so I smacked you. We are much better off to learn and live by self protection than we are self defense. We must teach our students

to be aware of their surroundings, to avoid trouble and to "mind set". We are doing our students a disservice if this isn't taught and talked about in every class. If we are only teaching self defense techniques we are failing them. Self defense is recovery from stupidity or bad luck.

K.I.S.S.

Keep It Simple, Stupid! In Krav Maga we want to have the fewest answers to the most questions. Our weapons defenses, especially, rely on simplicity. In our handgun defenses seminar we show a "cupping technique" that we learn for a handgun from the front that also works for handgun from the side of head, from a kneeling position, from a gunman in the guard, a gunman mounted, a gunman standing over us, a gunman across a bar or table...you get the picture. We have changed our long gun defenses so that one defense works from the front with the weapon aimed high, from the front with the weapon aimed low, with a slung weapon, from behind, etc. Same with our knife. We wrap the arm and beat on the attacker whether the attack is overhead, under/upward, straight stab, shank, slash, etc.

This is gold when we teach law enforcement officers...or anyone else for that matter. A lot of LEO's that we teach are mandated a whopping four hours per YEAR of unarmed training. They are not going to spend much time practicing what we show them...they have a lot of other things to do. To show them one defense that will work for several different attacks saves lives! They do not have to think of which defense works for that situation, didn't have to practice it much for it to come out of them and get good at the defenses with much fewer reps.

From time to time we get someone who believes that they have a much better stick, knife, long gun or handgun defense. I tell them that what they are showing me may well be better... but think about it. That defense you show me for, say, a handgun from the front may indeed be five percent better...a touch more effective, a touch quicker, etc. Now when you show me your handgun from the side and then from kneeling they are as different as night and day. Completely different muscle memory. Maybe one in sixty officers we teach are the type who love training, will spend hours working your different handgun defenses and get good with them. The other fifty-nine your five percent better defense made forty percent less safe! They won't practice, will hesitate when a handgun is shoved in their face thinking about which one of their twenty defenses they should use and will screw it up because they have so many defenses in their head.

Let's say you have a knife defense system that is just awesome but it takes 150 hours of work to be fairly proficient with it. What if on hour 148 someone puts a gun in my face? The only thing that we claim to do better in Krav Maga than anything else is to get people from zero to being able to defend themselves quickly. In four two hour seminars we can get people proficient enough in handgun, long gun, knife and stick to be able to defend themselves and live through an attack.

We are not in a Hollywood movie! We want to avoid flashy. Learning one simple defense with as few moving parts as possible that works in many situations saves lives. This is Krav Maga!

Mind Setting

Most self defense systems, martial arts, etc. fail to one extent or another in that they don't consider what effect real violence has on the one being attacked. As Winston Churchill said "No matter how enamored a commander is with their plans, from time to time one must consider the enemy." A real world attack will be at such speed (the attacker knew what was coming, you didn't), such close range and with such violence that it will overwhelm us. It is not uncommon for the person being attacked to just freeze. Mix in the fear of injury, the "this can't really be happening" thoughts and the fact that we may have taken damage and been dazed before we know what's going on and we are starting way behind the eight ball.

Mind Setting is the best thing that we can do to prepare for this random, sudden violence. Mind setting is rehearsing and visualizing actions in your mind. Military and Law Enforcement do this all the time. As violence in the U.S. seems to have skyrocketed in the past forty five years murders of police officers since the mid 1970's have decreased by 43%. This is attributed to what law enforcement started preaching and training at that time......Mind Setting (to be fair, our medical advances have helped with this as well). Mind Setting is making a plan for whatever the attack is. Officers started planning with their partners. "What will we do if at this stop light a gunman comes from your side, from behind, from my side?" "When we pull up to this house what will we do if a gunman comes out the front door, from the side, is behind us across the street?" Under stress and the dump our brains go to "animal" setting. We are not coming up with plans then. This is why tragedies like the Luby's restaurant massacre happen where people just sat in their seats and stared at the gunman as he went table to table and murdered over a dozen people. If we had a plan made beforehand it will surface!

For example, think about what you would do this evening if you were watching TV and someone were to kick in your front door, what you would do if you opened your eyes in bed at 2 a.m. to find someone standing over you, if you were suddenly surrounded by three large men in the parking lot at the mall, etc. etc.? Decisions about what you are going to do in a violent attack must be made well before the attack happens. The people who survive violent attacks are those who go off with rage....and do it immediately. When you are watching the news, reading the paper, etc. and come across a violent crime don't think "poor person" and move on or worse, "that couldn't happen to me". Think about exactly what you would do in that situation. I'm not talking about thinking how you will devastate four attackers with spinning high kicks (that is dreaming) but think about how you can escape (either right away I am running or I will smash this guys face and then run....if i am blocked i will kick and punch and hit with anything i can find on the ground until i can get out of there, etc.). Go over and over "what would i do" for every situation possible. If you think it can't happen to you, you won't plan for it. The U.S. government's own Justice department states "Every U.S. citizen now has a realistic chance of being a victim of random violence."

When attacked Mind Setting gives us the "been here, done that" feeling and gets us moving into action. When mind setting 1) visualize being in the crime. Not watching....in the crime. 2) visualize your actions to escape and 3) visualize being shot or stabbed or hurt in some way and still escaping.

Why Krav? We do drills at the end of every class. They suck because they wear us out but these drills are the most important thing we do in class. Think about it, in a drill we are being the victim of an attack. There are usually two or more partners pushing us, we are fighting back, we are going all out, etc. This is Mind Setting.....but doing it physically. When attacked in real life by two or more the "been there, done that" comes out as we have indeed been there and done that!!

The Freeze

The freeze is a very common phenomenon reported by those who have faced real violence... and is totally ignored by most self-defense systems. It will happen! There are a couple of things that cause this "freeze."

1) When a violent, stressful situation happens that puts you in extreme fear for your life your brain will work for you. If you have not trained for the attack, or had never even thought about the situation possibly happening, your brain will look at the violent attack and literally scan your entire life to see if this situation has ever happened before and how you got out of it. This is why you have heard people say "my whole life passed before my eyes." It does this faster than any computer but it takes a few seconds. Earlier we learned about mind setting. For facing real world violence mind setting is priceless. If we have planned for this encounter the plan will surface quickly. An interesting quote from Meditations on Violence by SGT Rory Miller..."The closer the events reflect previous experience, the less time it takes to orient. If the event is completely new there is nothing in the past to orient to, which explains the effectiveness of Judo in 1888, Jujutsu in America in the 1920's, Karate in the 1950's and BJJ in the 1990's."

This explains the phenomena of restaurant shootings where people just sit at their tables staring at a gunman walking around shooting person after person instead of running, throwing something, fighting back or doing anything at all. They do not have a plan and under extreme stress they go to midbrain and cannot come up with a plan. They sit there with their brains scanning and freezing.

2) Almost as bad as no training, as far as the freeze is concerned, is the wrong training. There is something called "Hick's Law" which states that the more options you have, the longer it takes to choose one. I remember reading an advertisement for a martial art that bragged that they had 7,000 different techniques! What kind of selling point is that? If you have more than one choice in an attack your brain has to choose one! Another example of the wrong training is techniques that are too regimented. If you train a defense that has six steps and it derails at step number two you have a hard time reorienting because the plan isn't being followed as you practiced.

Why Krav Maga? What makes Krav Maga such a great real world self-defense system is that it isn't technique based, it is philosophy based. As one of my instructor's loved saying years ago "if I learn 1,000 techniques, with my luck, I will go out on the street and be attacked by number 1,001." We want our first reaction, our "flinch" reaction, to be GO FORWARD AND GO HARD. When the surprise violence starts, when most people are freezing, we want our reaction to be to go forward with great violence...we don't want to even think about it. Our drills, everything we work on in our training and our whole philosophy is to keep it simple, to go right now and to make it as violent as possible when our lives are on the line. This isn't what I call brutal; this is what I call effective! Your only chance in a real life deadly encounter is to go right away and to go hard. When the blade is cutting you and you can't figure out why or from whom we want you to be able to automatically switch from confusion to absolute rage with the only thought running through your head to be "take down the scumbag!!"

The Dump

"We will fight like we train only if we train blind, numb, clumsy and stupid."
—SGT Rory Miller

We've all felt the effects of the adrenalin dump (actually a whole cocktail of hormones and chemicals, not just adrenalin). Something scares us (like a close call in our car) that leaves us tingling, breathing faster, heart rate up, etc. If this happens in an almost accident imagine how much more pronounced it will be with life threatening violence. This will happen and, sadly, this is something that is totally ignored in most self defense systems. Too many martial arts and defense systems take a logical and mental approach to visceral and chaotic problems.

Effects of fear (the "dump") include:

- your mind will change! The mind you have will not be the one fighting for you when attacked. Memories can be wildly distorted. Perception and auditory input can become very messed up. This is seen when those being attacked remember, for example, a knife that was four inches long being a machete, a handgun going off by their ear repeatedly that they didn't hear, etc. Irrelevant thoughts can intrude in our heads. Off the wall thoughts can seem like brilliant ideas. We make dumb decisions and get stubborn about them. We can get tunnel vision and not see the other attacker or the weapon. Behavioral looping can easily occur with trained fighters. They will use a technique that isn't working but get stuck on that technique and try it over and over. Sadly, if we haven't used mind setting and had a plan for this attack already formed we won't come up with one now because our mid-brain is now in charge and it will be stuck in freeze mode...trying to scan for any training for this scenario.

- You don't feel pain and don't bleed as badly due to vasoconstriction. This is one of the few good effects of the dump. Remember, however, that the attacker is in the same state and doesn't feel pain either. That awesome joint lock that you never fail with in class doesn't faze the bad guy....and we freeze because our brain said that it should end the fight.

- Skilled techniques degrade under stress....a bunch! Our heart rate goes way up. Blood is pooled into our internal organs. This makes our limbs feel heavy and we feel weak. Our skin gets cold and clammy. Fine motor skills go to pot.

The dump is the bane of Self Defense Instructors as it makes the untrained more dangerous and the trained less! A great example of this is police officers. When they are shooting at a target at the range within ten feet most have over 90% accuracy. Under fire on the street? One major city studied police hit statistics under live fire over a six year period and found that their officers from contact range to six feet out hit the bad guy only 38% of the time. There is a big difference in how our body reacts on a range and with someone actually trying to kill us!!

Again, the dump makes those who are trained fight worse....and the untrained actually fight better. Why is this? God put this response into man at the beginning. It wasn't for self defense but for self preservation against wild animals! No amount of technique will drive off a tiger, but a flailing, focused (tunnel vision), repetitive (behavioral looping) defense might. Not feeling pain and not bleeding like we usually would comes in handy when limbs are being bitten. At the worst stage we freeze, drop and even have bladder and bowel evacuation…..this is good as a last resort with a wild animal who may think you are dead and save you for later! If you ever hear someone say "if it were for real, I would have done a lot better" try not to laugh at them!

Why Krav? In our classes we don't teach a lot of joint locks or things that need fine motor skills? This is the reason! Under attack we want to think only of hitting the scumbag, grabbing hold of him any way we can and then kneeing and kicking him into oblivion. We don't teach that one devastating attack will end the fight…because when that technique doesn't end the fight we won't know what to do. We teach attacking with whole body, gross motor skills and we teach to go with all we have until they are on the ground, balled

You Will Get Hurt

Another subject most martial arts and self-defense systems fail miserably at is letting their practitioners know that they can and probably will sustain damage. This can be a game changer! If you rely on both hands to do a joint lock and break one…what do you do then? If we've never trained thinking about an injury and then it happens our brains want to freeze because this wasn't in the plan. If your instructor tells you "do our techniques right and you won't get hurt, the bad guy will" you probably need to look for another instructor!

What do you do if you use an art that does wrist locks and pressure points and the first thing that happens in an attack is your hand is crushed? What if you rely on jump kicks and high kicks and you break a leg? What if you were taught ballistic throws but your back goes out when you were tackled? In our higher level tests in Krav Maga we actually surprise our students by making them go an hour or two with an arm tied to their waist. We get to see all kinds of cool improvising…lots of head butts!

In our LEO seminars we tell our trainees that they will get hurt during an attack…they must think about this now, accept it and decide that when it happens they will pay back the scumbag one hundred times over. They do not have permission to quit no matter what! I am sure that you have all heard of the training where an officer who wasn't participating or paying attention gets shot with a blank and grabs where the bullet supposedly went in and falls to the ground. Hollywood and its stupid movies have built this fall down response into us. We will not do this. We know that a bullet doesn't have the force to knock us down and we have a lot of time to return fire or whatever else we need to do even if we did receive a damaging shot. We accept that there may be times that we get shot and we know that we will keep fighting. Go back to mind setting, plan for this to happen, see it happening and see yourself getting yourself and your partner out of danger.

Why Krav Maga? Any training that would include being injured on purpose would be short lived! We don't purposely injure anyone but we do go hard. Our drills don't cause injury but they do wear us out, make us feel like we can't go on and cause general discomfort. This is for a reason. We want to know that we can continue no matter what! Krav Maga's techniques are such that losing the use of a limb, in general, doesn't affect us. There are no joint locks or fine motor skill movements in our techniques but whole body, gross motor skills that we do in an extremely pissed off stage of mind...and we keep going until the bad guy is done!

Go Ahead, Get Mad

"The problem with most martial arts is that they take a logical and cerebral approach to a chaotic and visceral situation "
—SGT Rory Miller in MEDITATIONS ON VIOLENCE

"When things are at their darkest and it seems like there's no hope of surviving, well, that's when you gotta get mad dog mean"
—The Outlaw Josey Wales

Different "arts" and systems seem to take different approaches on how they view emotion. In sports fighting we are told that you can't fight mad, that you must be under control. Most martial arts preach Zen-like attitudes and to be calm under pressure. We root for the martial arts hero in the movies who seem calm and at peace as they whup butt.

These things just don't transfer to the real world. Fighting mad in sports makes you go hard and wear out...and you have several rounds to get through. The not fighting mad makes sense in that arena. The magical martial arts and their Samurai code are cool to study, great for self-discipline, fairly good exercise....and are fairly worthless when it comes to real violence.

When attacked on the street by a couple of scum bags who want to do you and your family harm going off with all the rage and hatred you can muster and fighting like an animal is the best chance you have of surviving. In SGT Samford Strong's must read book STRONG ON DEFENSE he interviews dozens of people who have made it through horrible, unimaginable crimes. His main points that come through again and again are that the people who survived these horrible attacks had two things in common. 1) They worried more about the crime being done to them than they worried about injury. They accepted injury and pain and decided to pay it back to the attacker ten-fold. 2) The ones who consistently fought back and won were those who went off with anger, hatred and rage.

The thought "how dare you think you are going to harm me, I will tear you apart" and then attacking like a wild animal has a much greater impact on survival than any techniques, system or art. We cannot worry about staying fresh for a prolonged fight as we want to destroy the attacker as quick as we can and get out of there. We certainly can't live by a "never strike first" or chivalrous code because the attacker's don't.

I tell student's all the time that Krav Maga will not save you, it is not magic. Mixing our techniques (which are easy to learn & remember, use gross, whole body motions and are designed to do as much damage as possible) with going off like a bomb brining out all the anger and rage you can muster is the best chance you have of surviving violence. Ask any law enforcement officer whom they would rather face; 1) a very proficient and talented martial artist or 2) some crazy who wants to claw off their face and chew on their eyes. They would much rather face the martial artist. If we can be both the crazy person and be proficient with our techniques we will be a scary opponent indeed.

We bring this out in our classes by not just learning techniques but by putting what we learn under stress and exhaustion. We run drills in our class that wear people out and make them want to quit. At that point it is all heart that gets them through it and heart on the street is worth more than any technique or system. We encourage people to yell and cuss during these drills. Not the "hiiiiii yaaaa" of those oh so controlled martial arts but we call the attacker a "son of a bitch", etc., etc. This may sound over the top but if we can see the scum bag in training, yell at him and hate him we are much, much safer on the street when it's for real and we have that "been there, done that" feeling.

The scum bags use violence as a tool, we must perfect that tool and wield it better than they do. If your butt is ever on the line get mad, get mean and fight with rage and hatred. It's the best chance you have. BE SAFE!

Be An Animal

The theme of many of my blogs has been that techniques don't save anyone...fighting with hatred and rage does. Fighting like an animal does. Krav Maga won't save you. Krav Maga with rage and going first, going hard & going forward will.

Freddie Roach Jr. tells the story of being attacked by three guys at once in his younger days. He dropped the first guy with a punch. The next two had him on the ground and were on top of him before he could react. He went "animal" and actually bit one of the guys' eyelids off. He says that he had eyelashes and skin in his mouth, actually thinks he bit the guys' eyeball.

It was over. The dude screamed and rolled off, his partner fled as well. The boxing technique saved him from the first guy, fighting like an animal saved his life.

From SGT Samford Strong's great book STRONG ON DEFENSE he talks about a horrible situation that was gotten out of by going "animal". He talks of a family camping in Mexico. Some local scum woke them up at night, got them all on their knees and had knives to all their throats. One of the scumbags made it apparent that he was planning on raping the nine year old daughter. Well, the mom went "animal". She grabbed the blade of the knife with both hands (surgery later) and went so ballistic that she actually got loose and in the confusion her husband also got loose. He went for his weapon he had in the tent and the whole family was saved. Mama didn't save them with any cool martial art or Krav techniques. She saved them by being an animal and being willing to fight to the death for her girl.

In the same book he talks about a woman who was awoken in bed by a man over her with a knife. She decided right then that she would rather die and that she would fight. Fight she did. She grabbed the blade of the knife (again, surgery later) and fought...not with any technique or training but like a cornered animal. She ended up doing some pretty major damage to the scum bag.

There is a beautiful illustration of this in Chuck Holton's book BULLET PROOF. The following is a couple of paragraphs from the book; "Capt. Brian Chontosh, found himself leading a patrol through the small town of Ad Diwaniyah, south of Baghdad. In what seemed like a single heartbeat, his unit was hit with a coordinated attack of mortars, rocket-propelled grenades, and machine-gun fire. Chontosh knew immediately that it was a near ambush...and that he and his men were in the kill zone. Retreat was not an option. Dying was.

But Captain Chontosh wasn't about to let that happen to his Marines. The love he felt for each of them instantly transformed into rage at those who would try to kill his men. He ordered the driver of his Humvee to plow directly into the enemy trench, and with a violence of action he leaped from the vehicle and attacked the attackers until his rifle ran out of ammo. He then pulled out his pistol and continued killing the enemy until that, too, ran dry. He picked up an enemy weapon and continued fighting. Then another. Then another. When it was over, more than twenty enemy fighters were out of commission and his men were saved." Capt. Chontosh didn't do what was expected. He didn't look for cover or run. He went "animal" and charged. That is what saved him.

I hope that we are learning that surviving real world violence isn't done by learning any marital art, self defense system, etc. if we are only learning techniques. We survive with heart. We go forward, go hard, go off and win no matter what. The scum bags use violence as a tool, we need to perfect violence and wield it better than they do. Be an animal to survive against animals.

Flawed Training

"Instructors, if you aren't putting everything you teach under stress and exhaustion you are teaching self defense techniques, not self defense. There is a big difference."
—M. Slane

Some self defense training is better than others but ALL training has flaws. The flaws are built in on purpose. Think about it, we are training to beat down someone until they are no longer a threat. How often do we do this in training? Never. It is truly like teaching people to swim but never getting in a pool. Now I am not advocating hurting each other in training. We must have built in flaws, but we must recognize that they are flaws.

The person attacking you in the gym is a partner who is there for your mutual benefit. They want you to be able to go to work tomorrow, want you to train with them next week, care about you and looks out for you. This is not the same person that will be attacking you on the street. When we accidently do make contact with our partner in the gym what is it that we usually do? We stop and apologize. This isn't the reaction we should be ingraining!

We train too often with pre conceived notions of what will work and what will happen in a fight. We get used to throwing three knees, dumping our partner to the ground and then starting the next rep. How do we know that those knees would have been devastating in a fight? He may well get up and come at us harder. In the real world people take pool cues to the head, stabs to the heart, multiple gunshots to the chest, etc. and keep coming. In training I've even heard students bawl out their partners with things like "I kicked you in the balls, you would have went down and been done". This may be a true statement but I'm not willing to bet my life on it.

In the gym we purposely pull our punches and kicks to not make contact. Again, what kind of training is that when the goal is to kick and punch people? If we pull our combatives 1,000 times in training under stress we will probably do exactly what we practiced. I knew a young man who practiced our headlock defense in class always smacking his partner's inner thigh instead of his groin. His partner appreciated it but he once had someone put him in a headlock on the street who was trying to hurt him and he did the defense...smacking the attacker on the inner thigh.

We fight in a gym that we keep open, padded and uncluttered for safety. When you're jumped the surfaces will be hard and there will be obstacles everywhere. The cop who is the USKMA's co-lead instructor, Brannon Hicks, swears he's gonna bring coffee tables and shrubs into his gym. He says every time he is in a fight one of those two things are in the way! The difference between a hazard and a gift is who sees it first. We need to train to see that curb or corner of the bar and use it…our gyms don't have these things!

We are told that we are training for life and death situations, forgetting about the in betweens. It could be life, it could be death, it could also be a colostomy bag, a wheelchair for life, blinded, brain damaged, etc., etc. We train with what Hollywood thinks is fighting in mind way too often! If we think about these other likely endings of a self defense scenario maybe we wouldn't be so macho, maybe we'd spend more time talking about how to avoid violence in the first place.

How do we mitigate the flaws in our training? The old adage "you fight like you train" is a lie unless (as SGT Rory Miller says in his books) you trained blind, deaf, stupid and clumsy. There is no great way to prepare for the chemical dump, emotions, freeze, etc. that a real world violent attack will create. We run drills to exhaust people and put them under some stress in our Krav classes but the student knows that they are in a class, they aren't really going to get hurt, they knew what was coming, etc. We cannot completely train for what is coming…that's just the way it is. Here are some things we do in our Krav classes to keep our training flaws at a minimum:

- Hit things hard…all the time! In our classes we spend the majority of our training time hitting focus mitts, kick shields, heavy bags, padded up people, etc. I have one rule in class when it's time to work combatives and that is once you have the technique down (and this is very soon after being introduced to it) you must always hit your hardest. If you are working punches, knees, kicks, etc. in my class I expect full out, knock someone the #$%^ out power. If you are pulling combatives and always going half power during training why would you expect to do it different under stress?

- Forget techniques. I don't have time in a real world violent attack to remember techniques. If I have a philosophy and a "flinch reaction" to go forward with rage, go hard and swing for the fences I will be much better off than working any technique. As Rory Miller says "100 counters to 100 attacks work for fighting, not for ambush…and it takes years to get good for that fighting. Techniques aren't important, what's important is training reflex." My awesome techniques do me know good if I haven't practiced for real world violence. I will freeze and take too much damage before any of those techniques come out of me.

- Train how you want to perform. Techniques will degrade under stress big time. If I am anal in training about keeping my chin down and head covered it will kinda come out of me under stress…if I was sloppy in training it won't come out at all under stress. Similarly, I don't warm up with shadow boxing, I warm up with shadow fighting. I am not teaching boxing. In boxing we throw a few combinations and then back out, circle, look for openings, etc. I do not want to do this in a violent attack as his buddy is coming to hit me from behind as I do all that dancing. I want to go forward throwing ten or twenty combatives and then get out of there. Which part of my training am I going to remember when under a real attack...the self defense or the dancing? I don't want to take the chance that I'll remember training that wasn't self defense so I avoid it!

- Exhaustion drills. These are the most important thing we do in our classes for self defense. Whatever we learned that day is going to be put under stress and exhaustion. If what you are using for self defense hasn't been put under stress and exhaustion how do you know it will work for real world violence? I can guarantee you that if you are fighting for your life there will be plenty of both stress and exhaustion. Think about how you are training, be honest about the Flaws.

Fight Dirty

"If you are in a fair fight, your tactics suck!"
—unknown

Every now and then I get comments about how fighting dirty isn't right. These comments always remind me about a group of martial artists that I overheard at a conference a few years ago. One of them told the others that Krav was just a system of cheap shots; that it had no honor and was basically cheating. This made me laugh out loud as I basically agreed with what they said but thought it was a good thing. One of my favorite all time qoutes on the subject comes from SGT Rory Miller's great book MEDITATIONS OF VIOLENCE. "Listening to the average martial artist talk about real world violence is like listening to ten year olds talk about sex."

When I teach new instructors I have a lecture I give about real world violence. One of the things that I talk about is that we aren't trying to instill a code of ethics, chivalry, honor or rules. If we have "honorable" rules like "never strike first", "never inflict more harm than needed", "always fight with honor", etc. we are putting our practitioners behind the eight ball. If the scum bags don't have rules we are hampering ourselves if we do. If the bad guys are going to use violence as a weapon we need to perfect that weapon and be more ruthless with it than the scum bags. If we are in a fair fight our tactics suck indeed!

When I hear talk about fighting right, with honor, etc. I know that whoever is saying it has no concept of real world violence and the kinds of human garbage that is out there preying on society. Here is a quote from a prison guard that I came across on the internet:

"Having these criminals on the streets should make you scared, very scared. If we don't have a means to defend ourselves from criminals, we are prey. I am not joking

by any stretch by telling you these criminals are animals. There are still those bleeding hearts who believe in the integrity of man and the desire to do the right thing when presented with a choice. I have now seen firsthand that there are people who are bad, and they are unfixable. They will take the low road every time, they will lie, steal, rape, murder and feel wholeheartedly that they are entitled to do whatever they please without respect to anyone else."

Yes, there are bad people out there who the world would be better off without. Read about the human pieces of crap that perpetrate home invasions. They are recidivists (hardened criminals who have been in prison for violent crimes and then let back out) who don't look at you and your family as humans but as entertainment. They will rape, torture and slaughter your family and then go have a hamburger. What honor and rules should you use if faced with these people?

Cheating, cheap shots and not fighting fair is the only way to survive a violent attack, especially when outnumbered or outgunned. One great example of this in history is The Battle of Stirling Bridge of the First War of Scottish Independence on 11 September 1297. William Wallace was vastly outnumbered and the enemy had much superior armor and weaponry. How did his force win? They cheated and fought dirty! At the time fighting honorably and fair meant that armies would allow each other to set up before battle. They would wait as the other army crossed a bridge, etc. and got completely set before the battle would begin. William Wallace's army attacked the English while they were crossing a long and narrow bridge and wiped them out. There was no honor in this. It was cheating and fighting dirty. They lived while the enemy died.

The only way to face ruthless, violent people and come away alive is to be more ruthless and more violent. This is why we do what we do in Krav Maga. Our classes, drills, testing, etc. is designed to get people past their breaking point and to make them ruthless, never say die, hard fighting, never quitting maniacs if they are ever in a life or death violent situation. BE SAFE!

S#!*'S About To Go Down

"Self Defense is recovery from stupidity or bad luck."
—SGT Rory Miller

We in the USKMA preach to avoid bad situations…don't go to stupid places with stupid people to do stupid things. Next we tell people to run when they see a violent situation. Thirdly, pick up something to use as a weapon and strike first if that's what it takes. Finally…use your Krav

Maga. You can see how far down the list actually using what we teach is. If you get to that point you missed some things!

In our instructor training, as well as our law enforcement training, we show a dash cam video of a law enforcement officer in a deadly force scenario with a big, belligerent man who tries to knife him. The scenario plays out and the cop ends up getting stabbed and shoots and kills the criminal. A sad ending that could have been avoided. We go through the video a second time showing the group how many signs the attacker gave that it was about to turn ugly. The officer misses five or six things that should have made him go hands on and diffuse the situation. Some are really obvious and makes you want to yell at the video!

We should be reacting as soon as we see a sign that an attack could be coming, not waiting for the actual attack. Hitting first is proactive. So is running. Waiting on the idiot to swing first is reactive and puts us behind the eight ball right off the bat.

Things the idiot in front of us will do to show his intentions (that aren't good) would include:

- Not listening. This is an obvious one that shouldn't be missed, but is. If a female (or anyone else) holds her hands up and says "don't come closer" and the idiot takes another step... this is a bad sign. She should kick him in the groin right then and there. Ignoring you and continuing to close on you is a bad sign.

- The person in front of you offsets his feet, one in front of the other and bases out. Why would you get in that stance? I do that when I'm going to hit something. It's hard to punch with my feet beside each other or close to each other.

- Face starts to flush, pulse visible and jumping in the neck, teeth clenched, forehead scrunching and fists start to ball. Any one of these should be a cue for us to do something. All at once is a sure sign that he/she's agitated and about to go off.

- Other signs of stress and agitation including voice getting higher & louder. Fast talking, increased breathing rate, restlessness, etc.

- Grooming. This is when the person you are having words with run the back of their hand across their nose, fingers through hair, wipe their brow, etc. This is a big sign. It generally means they just came to a decision on what they are going to do...and it caused stress. On the video when the criminal is coming across a highway railing he pauses, wipes his palm across his forehead, and then resumes. That was the exact moment he decided he would attack the officer.

- Standing bladed. You hide one side of your body when you don't want the person in front of you to see what you are doing on the other side…like accessing a knife.

- For law enforcement especially we talk about target glancing. If you are talking to someone who glances at your sidearm a few times…do something. He's about to lunge for it. If a suspect keeps glancing past you or behind them they are looking for a good path to run from you. If any of us see someone approaching and glancing back and around…look out. They are about to strike and are checking one last time to make sure there are no witnesses.

Watching out for any and all of these things will keep us safer. Realize why the person is acting the way they are and take appropriate measures. Avoid situation where you have to use Krav Maga…that's good advice!

2

Combatives

"Surviving violent encounters is a matter of mastering fundamentals, being meaner than a junkyard dog and getting lucky."
—SGT Brannon Hicks

We must learn proper combatives to make our weapon defenses effective. Most Krav Maga defenses follow RCAT. Redirect, Control, Attack and Takeaway. There is always a punch, elbow, kick, knee, etc. in our defenses to keep the assailant in the OODA loop, incapacitate them, etc. When in a life and death situation we must hit as hard as we possibly can. If we knock the idiot out our defense is over...and successful! Proper technique helps us to maximize power and keep our own injuries to a minimum.

Keep in mind that the "takeaway" part of RCAT isn't in stone. We must always take a handgun or long gun with us but do not have to disarm an attacker who has a knife or stick. We can create distance to escape or to access our own weapon in those cases.

Before we go over the straight punch technique a page from our Krav Maga for Law Enforcement book:

To Punch or Not To Punch

It is common training with law enforcement officers to teach palm strikes and avoid punching. Officers are told not to punch because 1) they can easily break their hand and not be able to access their handgun or other weapons and 2) punching is against a lot of department's policies. Well, for years I taught like everyone else and dissuaded law enforcement officers from punching. Then, out of the blue, I realized that I am an adult who can think for himself! If I believe something will keep officers safer, even if it's against conventional wisdom, I had better be teaching it.

Let's look at that number two reason first, it's against policy. I have heard of several departments that consider an officer punching to be a use of lethal force but for some illogical reason don't consider someone punching at their officers to be use of lethal force. I can certainly understand not punching in most instances but when an officer's life is on the line he or she must know that they have permission to punch! When the USKMA teaches law enforcement seminars we mainly deal with lethal force scenarios. We show handgun, long gun, knife and blunt object disarms. If an officer in that situation is legally allowed to fire on the assailant it is certainly legal for him or her to punch. A palm attack has to hit the assailant in the nose or throat to have much of an effect but a punch cuts and does tissue damage wherever it hits. When we punch during weapon disarms our goal is to knock out the attacker. It is much easier to knock someone out with a punch than a palm attack (or we would see the UFC fighters palming).

Now, about those hand injuries. You can certainly get a boxer's fracture from punching a skull but palming isn't exactly guaranteed to be injury free. If you throw a palm to a skull or torso you can sprain or otherwise injure your wrist fairly easily. While palming you can also catch your thumb wrong and tear the thumb ligament. A boxer's fracture isn't going to keep an officer from accessing and firing his handgun. He's not even going to feel it until much later when the adrenaline dump has dissipated. You would have to fracture most of the bones in your hand to keep from accessing and firing a weapon. Fractures from punching are almost always the metacarpal bones on the pinky side of the hand. The pinky doesn't have much of a function when firing a handgun. I had a boxer fracture years ago that I did at the beginning of a third degree black belt test in the martial art I was practicing at the time. I went on to test for a few hours afterwards and, other than pain, it didn't affect anything that I had to do with my hands.

I have had a few officers tell me that the reason they aren't allowed to punch is that if they break their hand it means six to eight weeks off of work and someone having to be paid overtime to replace them. This I believe!

When an officer's life is on the line he or she needs to know that they have permission to punch! We have to punch in training if we expect it to come out under stress.

Straight Punch

Straight punches are one of the main combatives in Krav Maga. Straight punches are powerful strikes that can go to the attackers head or body. Like all combatives, strive to hit with your entire body weight instead of just an arm.

The straight punch starts with the hips.

For the right punch the right hip turns sharply towards the target. We do this by pivoting on the right foot as if putting out a cigarette. Next, the right ribs turn towards the target and, finally, the hand is sent straight towards the target. Do not "muscle" (tense) the arm. The body turn provides the power and the hand is sent like snapping a towel. The torso stays upright throughout the punch as if a rod were inserted down through the puncher's spine.

Make sure that the hand comes from face level to the target and is returned back to the face. The hand never drops to show the attacker a target. Do not drop your hands or follow through so far that you open up your face. Think about punching over a fence to where you cannot drop the hand at all. Do not leave the hand out after a punch but bring it back to fighting position as fast as it went to the target.

We are attempting to have our chin protected behind the shoulder of the punching arm. Our other hand stays up to protect from a counter-attack. Hips and body turn to generate power in the punch. The fist is closed with thumb wrapped around the outside. First two knuckles align with the radius (inner forearm bone) for support and strength.

Palm Heel Strikes

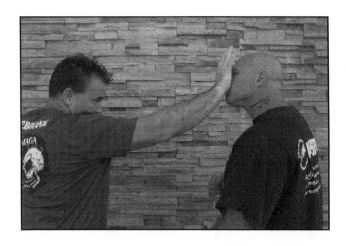

With palm heel strikes the targets are more specific than with punches as a palm to the cheek doesn't have the impact of a closed fist. Aim for under the nose or the throat. Palm strikes are better for pushing off or stopping as in palming an attacker's face who is attempting to head butt you. The palm heel strike is the exact same motion as a punch. The striking area is the bottom of the palm, the heel.

Elbows

Elbows are sharp, pointy surfaces that are used to strike targets at a close range. Elbow strikes are not just swinging an arm but, as in all combatives, a whole body motion.

To the Front

Push off with the same foot as the striking elbow to get the entire body weight behind the strike. At the point of impact, the forearm is parallel with the ground; chin is down with the striking arm protecting the face. The swing isn't across the target but forward, burying the point of the elbow straight into the target. Do not step through after contact but stay in the same stance you started in. This keeps the attacker in front of you for the next series of strikes.

To the Side

An attack from the side is generally a surprise, or is noticed only at the last second, not leaving time to turn and square up to the opponent. Therefore, practice this strike from a neutral stance or from fighting an opponent that is in front of you as his partner is coming in from the side. Push off the foot opposite the striking arm, bringing the arm as far across the body as possible. Launch toward the attacker, getting the full body weight behind the strike. The striking arm stays high enough to protect the chin (looking like Count Dracula holding his cape over his face), as the other hand comes up to protect the face from the other side. Finish turning into the attacker to finish.

To behind, around

Look first to see the target. Aim for the side of the neck or head. Whip the torso around as the arm is raised high enough to cover the face. Be sure to strike with the point of the elbow, not the tri-cep. There is no step with this strike unless needed for distance. Always remember; your hands are faster than your body, your body is faster than your feet. If you are stepping you are slowing down the technique. Strike and then turn into the attacker to finish.

To behind, straight back

Send this strike straight back to the xiphoid or groin, or bend forward at the waist to target the attacker's chin. Shoot the hand forward as far as possible then send the point of the elbow straight back. There should be no gap between body and arm as the arm passes the ribs.

Strike Defenses

If a system has a different defense for a blade than it does for a punch it is a bad system. Ask any police officer you know and they will tell you that the majority of people who they have seen stabbed thought that they were being punched. We certainly can't take the time to see what's in the attacker's hand before we react. A punch defense must also work for a knife, one defense that we react with.

Outside (360°)

Any strike that comes from the outside, from any angle, is fairly easy to meet as it is a natural reaction to get an arm up in the way. It is also, unfortunately, natural to back away from the strike. Krav Maga takes natural motions and adds aggression to them so get the body behind the block and go into the attack. The blocking hand should be open to maximize blocking surface. Meet the attack at a 90° angle so as to stop the attack, not redirect it to slide down the arm and hit another area of the body. If the attack is recognized early enough, burst in off of your back foot as the defense is made, catching the striking appendage as far back as possible. Strike at the same time with the opposite hand.

Inside

In a ready stance, any punch coming to the face must come through the circle made by the hands. To defend a right punch, extend the left hand at a 45° angle a few inches. The base of the defender's thumb rides down the arm of the attacker, deflecting the punch away from the face. Also make a slight head defense by moving the head behind the blocking hand.

The movement should be small and simple as if attempting to poke the attacker's eyes. Do not slap straight across as this would open you up for a second punch. Make sure your hands are high enough to not have to raise them before defending; this is too slow to adequately defend. Also make sure the hands are far enough from the face to make a small movement with the hands have a large impact on the path of the punch.

Low

This is a defense against a punch or stab to the body or groin. As the punch comes, squat to the level of the punch and snap the front arm across the body, turning the palm in toward your face. The defense is a combination of turning the body and snapping the arm across. Be sure to keep the forearm straight up and down, at a 90° angle to the floor, not chopping or swiping down. Chopping down takes the knife from hitting your mid chest to hitting your groin…neither make for a good day! This defense is the beginning for a straight stabbing knife defense to the midsection so it is important to always use the front arm, so as to redirect the weapon as quickly as possible.

Kicks

Front Kick

The front kick is sent, more often than not, to the groin by aiming anywhere in the "A frame" that an attacker's legs form. Snap the hips forward, send a slightly bent leg upward, and snap the knee right before contact. Don't chamber (load up to the back) the leg before the kick, as this slows the kick and telegraphs the movement to the opponent. It is not important to be concerned with what part of the leg connects, as anything from the big toe to the knee is an effective striking tool against the groin. After the kick, land forward on the kicking foot to go in and strike again.

Stomp Kick

This kick is used to knock someone backwards and off balance by hitting the chest, or to double them over by hitting below the waist. Bring your back leg's knee to the chest and "punch" with the bottom of the foot. Make sure to snap the hips forward (as with throwing a knee) when "punching" with the foot.

Foot Stomp

This is a very effective, easy to do motion. Simply raise a knee as high as possible and stomp down with the heel, as if crushing a pop can. The top of the foot is a good target, especially if being bear hugged from behind. Other targets are the side of the lower leg at an angle (to snap the tibia and fibula bones) or, if the attacker is getting up from the ground, the same angle on the arm will snap the radial and ulna bones. Coming down on the Achilles tendon with this kick is called a "hobble". Even on drugs they won't be able to chase you down as this causes structural damage. In a life-threatening scenario, this can also be used to the back of the skull.

Knee Strikes

Knee in the fight

To throw a proper knee in the fighting stance, stay back from the opponent in a good stance. Lean the upper body back (as if to lay on the ground) and shoot the hips forward with power. Kneeing this way gives a lot more travel distance to get momentum going and has the pointed knee cap the striking surface.

Kneeing from the side clinch

Grabbing and kneeing is very effective. Grab hold of the neck and tri-cep on the same side of the head with a strong grip, leaving "cow bites" on the attacker's neck, arm and/or shoulder. Dig the fingers in. If not, the attacker will just slap your hands off. Grabbing tightly enables the person kneeing to pull the attacker into the knee strike. The stance must stay deep as you put your weight on the attacker to keep the attacker from reaching the hips. Elbows are bent pointing to the ground to keep the attacker's head and neck misaligned. When the knee is thrown, quickly straighten the arms and lean back, bursting the hips forward. Strike with the knee and get back into a deep stance immediately so as not to be pushed off balance. When throwing multiple knees, stay in a deep stance in between each knee. Between knees, try to pull and push the attacker to keep him/her off balance. The attacker cannot strike back as easily if he/she doesn't have balance.

Knee spike

This is a useful technique in some weapon defenses as well as used for a takedown. It can be described as walking with force while raising the knees high or, as one instructor has described it "Stepping over a log with anger." The plant foot (outside foot) steps towards the attacker, even with the attacker's stance. Strike the opponent's back thigh (near the hip) with the other knee. This is to knock the attacker off balance to continue counter attack or to take to the ground. In training, it is easy to hurt the pad holder with this strike. Have the pad holder hold the tombstone pad against the top of the back leg/pelvis and not put weight on that leg. Take the first few reps slowly. This technique is also used when "attached" i.e.: grabbing the attacker's shirt lapel, neck, etc. using this to pull the attacker to the ground as the displacement knee is delivered.

TRAIN TO REACTION: Learning 100 defenses to 100 attacks may work with sparring, after years of practice, but it will not work for ambush. In our seminars he has everyone work on a "reaction" to any attack. If something comes at us we must just react with one movement that we can rely on to defend/attack whatever is coming at us. Rory Miller, in his seminars, teaches to enter with a "spear"…lunging in with an elbow that is high enough to cover his face (great idea). We in Krav Maga work on a simultaneous block and strike so what I am entering with is a lunge into a punch with my right hand while getting the left up to block whatever is thrown, followed by a knee to the groin. I practice this with a partner who, as soon as they lung, throw a punch, kick, etc. I can react to. Get in while blocking and striking at the same time…react to everything the same and there is no "freeze" time while I think of the defense for what they are throwing.

3

Edged Weapon Defenses

"Self defense is recovery from stupidity or bad luck."
—SGT Miller

Knives are the last thing I want to come across on the street. Knives are a danger because they are concealable (most who get stabbed never saw the knife, they thought they were being punched), everyone has one, small angle changes in the attack make for large angle changes in the defense and any idiot can kill you with one. Also, think about the mindset. A handgun is a distance weapon. A timid attacker can just close their eyes and pull the trigger. Someone with a knife wants close, wants to see you bleed. I'll take a very competent and well trained martial artist as an assailant over a nutso with no training but the desire to kill any day!

A handgun has a reach advantage over the knife, this is obvious. At close range, the only advantage the firearm has is the POSSIBILITY of greater damage per strike. A knife has far more advantages over the handgun at close range including 1. Unlimited use, never have to reload. 2. It doesn't require aiming. 3. It can cause damage at ANY angle of attack. 4. It is more difficult to control a knife as the defender. 5. It can be used stealthily, often the victim doesn't know it's in use until it's too late.

TRAINING TOOLS: The training tool that is popular with Krav people that I don't get are the shock knives. They don't hold up that well, are expensive and…pretty friggin worthless in my opinion. What is the reason to use shock knives (or the old put lipstick on a rubber knife and wear a white t shirt)? Are you saying that if you get touched by the knife you didn't do the defense right? I call bullshit on that. In a knife attack you are going to get cut. We don't even call it "knife defenses" in our seminars, we call it "knife survival". If you are doing defenses and not getting touched by the knife I can guarantee you that the attacks aren't realistic. We expect to get cut, we are trying to avoid the 40 stab wounds to the chest that the average psycho is attempting to deliver. I've also been told that the "shock" mimics pain and teaches us to keep going when we feel it. I would suggest that people who believe that go study the adrenaline dump and stress. You ain't feeling pain under the stress of someone trying to kill you…that comes later!

A much better training tool for knife defenses would be KY jelly. Any defense you are teaching should be able to be used with that stuff slathered all over your arms and hands. There is blood on the scene of almost every knife attack. Blood is one slippery substance. If the defense can't be used effectively all slicked up like that it isn't a good defense. Guess what, most every defense you know for a knife fails under that test. What works best? Punching or kicking the attacker as hard as you can as you attempt to block the blade…and creating distance to get the heck out of there or access a better weapon.

Now, let's talk about "realistic" attacks. When most self defense experts talk about a realistic attack they are talking about a shank, hockey punch or the like type of attack. Actually, I would argue that. Any of the attacks listed in this chapter, including someone coming from ten feet away, have happened. Whichever swing or distance a person gets attacked with certainly seems realistic to them! My problem with the defenses I learned in martial arts was that they all started half way across the room. Can that happen? Of course. Should we also train for stabs that happen with someone starting who is already right up against us? Of course.

If I were a scumbag and wanted to do great bodily harm to someone with a knife I would blitz the person, hit them hard and push them back while keeping the knife out of reach in my strong hand and pushing, punching, controlling their limbs with my off hand. What technique works for that? Our "hockey punch" defense is the closest thing we have technique wise but, thankfully, we are philosophy based. We would teach to blitz the attacker, swing for the fences punching them in the throat and kicking them in the groin all the while keeping an arm in the way to block the knife. The philosophy is to not get stabbed (block) and to knock out the idiot. Nothing else to remember, no technique to recall. Just be brutal and hurt the idiot trying to stab you!!

Disengage

The first technique to work on in knife defense training is simply to create distance. When the partner who is playing the attacker reaches for his pocket simply retreats at an angle, draw your own weapon if you are carrying or run away. The second technique is started a bit closer. As the attacker reaches for his pocket punch the attacker in the soft part of the face (a workout partner is holding a focus mitt with their left hand across their body, beside their head) and then run or back off at an angle to access your own weapon.

Side step kick

This is a defense for a straight or overhead stab that starts from a good distance away.

1) As the stab is coming (from a right handed attacker) step at a 45 degree angle with your right foot to get offline and…

2) Deliver a front kick to the attacker with your left. The kick is to the groin if the attacker is upright, to the face if he is bent over leading the attack with his head.

3) After the kick create distance or deliver combatives, whichever the situation calls for.

Switch kick

1) As the attacker is delivering a straight stab (with right hand) "skip" step to your right side, ending up with your left foot slightly in front of where your right foot started.

2) With your right foot deliver a front kick to the face (if the attacker is bent and coming in low) or a roundhouse to the back of the attacker's knee. This isn't a jump but a skip step, both feet are off the ground at the same time. If there were a ceiling one inch above your head the ceiling wouldn't be touched.

3) Continue to create space or deliver combatives at the end.

Bailing round house

The attacker is delivering a straight stab (with right hand).

1) Burst off of your right foot to your left side with your left foot landing as far outside as possible and pointed away at a ninety degree angle from the attacker. Your body is parallel to the floor as you…

2) Stretch away from the blade and deliver a roundhouse with the ball of your right foot to the groin.

3) Create space or deliver combatives after the defense.

Knife held, static

When you are threatened with a knife held on you statically revert to handgun defenses. Cupping defense for knife held in front, gun from behind defense if held at your back, etc. Keep in mind to grab the wrist and not the blade.

  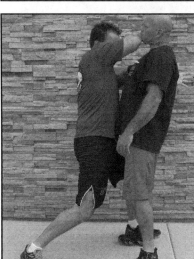

Sudden straight stab, hands up

By sudden we mean from a fairly close range and you didn't see the attack until the very last second. If your hands are up:

1) Swat downward and hook the knife hand as you deflect the knife away from your body.

2) Simultaneously push, punch or throw a front kick to the groin and then disengage, make space and draw your own weapon or run away

This isn't necessarily a technique but a reaction. Swat, throw a combative and make distance between yourself and the attacker

Sudden straight stab, hands down

The same as above but you were caught with your hands down.

Slap the knife with fingers pointed to the ground (using the palm to contact the attacking hand) and punch or throw a kick/knee spike and then disengage, make space and draw your own weapon or run away.

Sudden stab from extreme angle, straight, overhead or underhand

When the sudden stab from a right handed attacker comes from your right side the angles change so that after blocking you will end up on the dead side.

Block with an outside defense and kick to the knee as you begin to create distance. The kick is done in passing as you are fleeing and if missed simply keep creating distance.

Straight stab

Your hands are up as the attacker lunges in.

1) Take your left forearm (if a right handed attack) and block down on the knife hand. "Hollow out" with your body as you block.

2) Continue after the redirection with your forearm wrapping the attacker's arm and burst in with a knee to the groin as you control the knife arm by wrapping it with both of your arms. You are bursting in as you wrap the arm, not standing in one place and reaching.

3) Keep hold of the attacker's arm to control the knife while simultaneously delivering knees and front kicks to the attacker.

4) Wrap the attacking arm and throw combatives until the attacker is unconscious or you can push off and get away. If a disarm is needed snap your left shoulder forward to get the attackers knife hand in front of you then reach with your right hand to put your fingers over theirs. Twist the knife more in front of you with your right and grab the wrist with your left. Use a cavalier as the takeaway (turn hand like a door knob as you hold it in place, snap down and dig knife out of palm).

Alternate ending, head pass

1) Take your right hand and grab the back of the attacker's head/neck. Push the head down and through across your body as you take a short, sharp step backwards with the left foot. This spins the attacker to where he/she is facing away from you and has them sitting on the ground, then to lying on the ground.

2) Then place both hands on the wrist to control the blade as you can either stomp on the attacker from a standing position or put your shins on the attacker's head and body while tightly squeezing their arm between your thighs. The knife can then be twisted out of their hand, combatives can be thrown or our own weapon can be deployed.

Overhead stab

1) As the knife is raised overhead by the attacker burst in with an outside defense to the upper with your left hand (assuming a right handed attack) and punch with your right. This is the only part of the defense needed if the punch moves the attacker away from you. Simply retreat and draw your own weapon or run away.

2) Continue after the redirection with your forearm wrapping the attacker's arm and burst in with a knee to the groin as you control the knife arm by wrapping it with both of your arms. You are bursting in as you wrap the arm, not standing in one place and reaching.

3) Keep hold of the attacker's arm to control the knife while simultaneously delivering knees and front kicks to the attacker.

4) Keep the wrap on the attacking arm and throw combatives until the attacker is unconscious or you can push off and get away. Because the angle of this attack has us wrapping with over hooks it is not easy to get to the wrist for a takeaway. We can pivot sharply on our left foot as we hold onto the arm tightly and snap the elbows of the attacker with our body.

Underhand stab

1) As the knife comes from the ground upward apply an outside defense downward with your left arm (assuming a right handed attacker) and at the same time strike with your right

2) After the block go in with a flying knee as you wrap the knife wielding arm with your left arm ending up with their arm held tightly against your body. Bear hug both arms and throw combatives.

3) Keep the wrap on the attacking arm and throw combatives until the attacker is unconscious or you can push off and get away. During the combatives you can switch grasp when safe to do so by wrapping with left arm and pushing head away with right palm (assuming a right handed attacker). If a takeaway is needed curl your left arm to bring the knife in front of you and then put your right hand's fingers over their fingers and take away with a cavalier (pulling the wrist with your left hand as you push with your right, bending their hand behind their arm in a direction that it doesn't want to go).

Hockey Punch

This attack is when the assailant grabs an arm and then stabs over and under that arm. You must do three things simultaneously with all your might. 1) Block the knife, 2) attack the attacker with punches, elbows, knees, kicks, etc. and 3) keep pressure on the attacker by going in and pushing him/her backwards. Strike as hard as possible until you can break the grip then retreat or draw your own weapon.

Shank

1) A shank can come from any angle, any side. Locate the attacker and burst to the arm pit to wrap up the attacking arm with both of your arms.

2) As you grasp the arm throw combatives at the attacker

3) Throw combatives until the attacker is unconscious or you can push off and get away.

4) If a takeaway is needed curl your left arm to bring the knife in front of you and then put your right hand's fingers over their fingers and take away with a cavalier (pulling the wrist with your left hand as you push with your right, bending their hand behind their arm in a direction that it doesn't want to go).

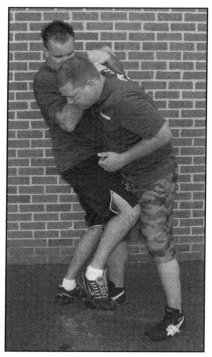

Slashing

If you catch the slash on the swing from out to in simply defend with the overhead or underhand defense (depending on the height and angle of the attack).

1) If the attacker has slashed from out to in and is on the way back with the knife (in to out) pivot on your right foot (assuming a right handed attacker) so that you get deep into the attacker with fingers pointed to the sky, building a wall with your forearms. (as an aside, you should block with the back of the arms. There are more arteries, etc. that can be damaged if cut on the front of the arm. Even with that truth we generally block with the front of the arms as this is a natural motion that will come out of us. Nobody, when startled, turns their palms towards themselves).

2) After blocking the attacking arm pivot out on your right foot as you take your left arm and ballistically point the arm to the ground, passing the knife to the attacker's right side.

3) Wrap the attacking arm and throw combatives until the attacker is unconscious or you can push off and get away. If a takeaway is needed curl your left arm to bring the knife in front of you and then put your right hand's fingers over their fingers and take away with a cavalier (pulling the wrist with your left hand as you push with your right, bending their hand behind their arm in a direction that it doesn't want to go).

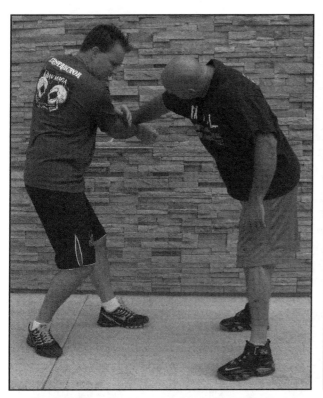

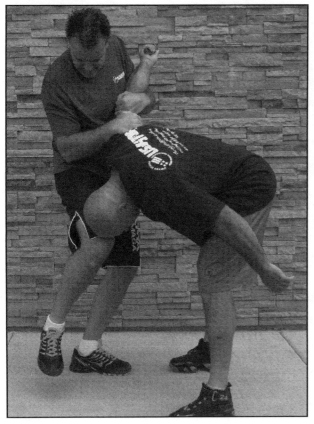

Knife to the throat from front (and against wall)

The way I see this defense generally taught scares me to death. It is generally taught to is to bring your hand across and take the knife off to the side. My question is how in the world to you know which way the blade is pointed. If it is pointed to the right and I take it off to the left I will slice my own throat. I can't see it, it's below my chin. Even if the attacker's knuckles and the blade are against my throat how do I know the difference in feel of his/her knuckles at the base of their fingers and the knuckle at the first joint as they bend their fingers? Under stress if I do this defense I will have a fifty percent chance of slicing my own throat!

Much better is to:

1) Raise arms, grab one hand's fist with the other hand and slam down hard on the arm that is holding the knife, as if hugging the attacker's arm quickly with great force.

2) Chop step backwards to pull the attacker off balance as you twist your body back and forth, shaking the attacker's arm like a dog shaking a rag.

3) Throw knees and front kicks at the attacker.

4) Throw combatives until the attacker is unconscious or you can push off and get away.

If against a wall puff your chest and look up as you grab the arm. You cannot step backwards but at an angle along the wall.

Knife to the throat from behind

1) Explosively dig the fingers of both hands over the attacker's forearm and grab deep on the forearm finishing with your hands between your chest and their arm.

2) Grab and roll the arm down your chest to get the knife off of your throat.

3) Step with your left foot (if right handed attacker) between your right foot and the attacker.

4) Get your head to the back of the attacker, keeping their arm pinned to your chest. You are now facing the side of the attacker where you can push off with your right foot over and over, plunging the knife into the attacker's side while continuing to hold the arm tight to your chest or you can control the knife arm and throw combatives until the attacker is unconscious or until it is safe to push off.

Behind, shoulder held (left and right turn)

This is a hostage type situation where you are being led to another location. The attacker has the knife in your back and a hand on your shoulder. If the shoulder being held is your left you can only turn right. As you turn to your right this defense is very similar to the hostage knife to the ribs.

1) After redirecting the knife with the back of your right arm finish the turn and push on the attacker's elbow with your left hand to keep the knife hand from being able to pull back.

2) Wrap your right arm around the attacker pinning the knife hand under his/her arm pit, hugging the attacker tightly to keep the forearm pinned between your bodies. Strike with knees and head butts until you can push away and escape or

3) Grab the attacker's wrist in the crook of your right arm and pivot on your left foot, put your left hand as a wall to the attacker's elbow as you turn and snap the attacker's elbow.

 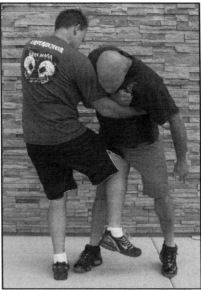 

If your right shoulder is being held you must turn left. The defense is similar to the handgun from behind.

1) Turn left and burst in wrapping the attacker's arm with your left while punching or elbowing the face with your right.

2) Keep the attacker's arm wrapped and throw combatives and push off or grab the knife hand fingers over fingers and cavalier the wrist for a takeaway.

 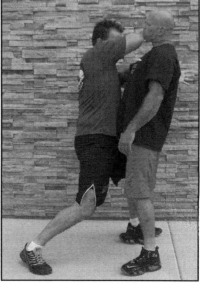

Hostage, against wall, knife at distance

1) Perform the "choke against the wall" technique by raising your right arm putting your bicep on the ear (assuming a right hand attacker with left hand pinning you against wall).

2) Staying on the wall turn your body towards your right, breaking the attackers grip.

3) You are on the attacker's dead side. Push off and escape or attack the attacker's dead side with combatives. Be aware that you are not controlling the knife so aim for vital areas and hit hard, always ready to wrap the knife holding arm when it presents itself.

ANOTHER OPTION: Shoot your right arm down and wrap the arm holding your throat or shirt and pivot towards the wall, bending the attacker's arm backwards. Snap the elbow and push off or clinch for combatives.

YET ANOTHER OPTION: If you feel that you are stronger than the attacker you can push off the wall, block at the attacker's bicep and throw combatives.

Hostage from behind, knife in ribs

1) Assuming a right handed attacker turn ballistically to your right, redirecting the knife off of your body and pinning it against the attacker's body with the back of your right arm.

2) Continue to turn taking your left hand to the attacker's right elbow and keeping pressure on the elbow so that the arm cannot pull the knife back.

3) Keeping the left hand on the attacker's right elbow bear hug the attacker with your right bicep pinning the knife hand into the attacker's left arm pit.

4) Throw knees and front kicks to the attacker's groin.

5) Move your right hand to the front of the attacker, catching the knife holding hand's wrist between your forearm and bicep.

6) Pivot ballistically on your left foot while placing your left hand like a wall at the attacker's elbow. This will bend the attacker's elbow back and hyperextend it or even break it.

7) You can put your body into the attacker's arm pit and raise your left leg as you sit forcing the attacker's face into the ground as you fall or simply hug the attacker's arm by the wrist with your left arm as you peel the knife out of their hand with your right.

Knife, attacker in guard

If the attacker had sense they would sit back and slash at the arteries on the inside of your upper let but every video we have seen of this attack the attacker is leaning in and trying to stab the victim's face and upper body. Either way:

1) As you block place your left shin across the attacker's pelvis/abdomen.

2) Push off with the shin and start to kick the attacker with your right leg.

3) Start "riding the bike with anger" as you stomp and kick the attacker with both legs

4) Get to your feet as soon as possible to continue attacking or escape.

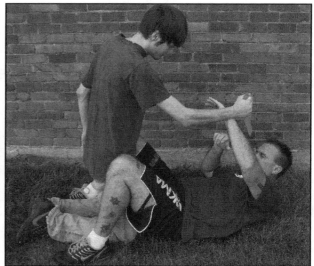
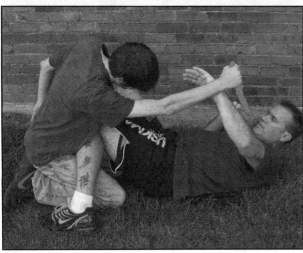

Knife; mounted

1) We must block the blade and attack the attacker with fists and elbows to the groin and head. At this same time we buck to keep the attacker off balance and not being able to hit what he is aiming for.

2) As you attack and block you are bucking to get the attacker to base out. When they base out (put the knife holding hand to the ground) wrap the wrist with your arm tightly against your chest.

3) After wrapping the wrist continue to attack as you buck and roll while controlling the knife hand so that you end up on top where you will continue to attack until you can safely get up.

The time to buck and roll is the split second you wrap and control the knife hand as that hand is being pulled to the ground and the attacker's weight is shifting forward.

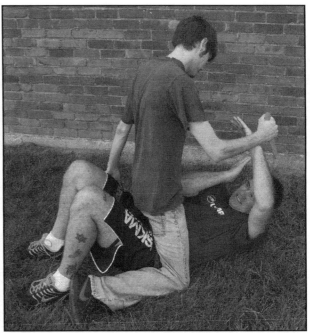

Knife, attacker mounted knife at throat

1) Raise arms, grab one hand's fist with the other hand and slam down hard on the arm that is holding the knife, sliding the arm down your body and knife away from your throat.

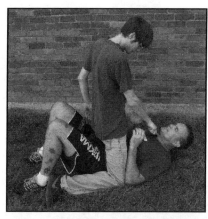
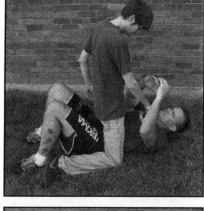

2) Assuming a right handed attacker, buck and roll to your left.

3) Throw combatives, get both hands on the knife wielding arm and pin to attacker or ground as you continue to throw combatives.

4) Pushing on the attacker's arm pop up to your feet while keeping weight on the arm and push off of the attacker as you create distance.

Seminar: Edged Weapon Defenses (2 – 2 ½ hours)

- Show videos of wounds and attacks.
  http://www.youtube.com/watch?v=9lTcI1AHfqU
  http://www.youtube.com/watch?v=DNOP3X9OyzM

- Talk about dangers of knife: Why we would rather face a handgun on me than a knife:

  1) Concealable…majority stabbed thought they were being punched; 2) small angles on attack need large angles on our defense; 3) everyone has one (80% carry..look next time in mall); 4) any idiot can kill you with one; 5) mind set…gun is distant. Idiot with a knife wants to get close, see you bleed. I would rather face a technical fighter than one with the will to kill.

1) Weapons of convenience. Show them to push legs of chair/fire extinguisher, etc. at the attacker and kick under. Drill this with two pads. Attacker holds for front kick while defender pushes pad into attacker's chest (pretending it's that chair, fire extinguisher, etc.) and kicks under it. Do not let them pull striking pad out of the way to kick but kick under it.

2) Attacker reaches for pocket. First at a distance–run. Then a bit closer – Punch focus mitt held representing face then run.

3) Attacker swings overhead attack. Block with an outside block and punch at same time. Create distance and run.

4) Line drill. Line of attackers with knife swing and student blocks/punches one after the other.

5) Overhead stab. Outside defense with strike, wrap arm with under/over and start combatives. Then with realistic attack (sewing machine needle) throwing attacker to the ground or pushing off after a few combatives, retreat or continue with combatives. Then show head pass takedown. Contact shot when available.

   Straight stab 7)Under hand stab 8) Shank defense 9) Slash

   10) From front knife held to throat 11) From behind knife to throat 12) Attacker mounted

   13) Attacker in guard 14) Hockey punch attack

   15) DRILL; any attack, with KY jelly slathered on arms

 67

LINE DRILL: One practitioner is defender and the rest of the group are in a line, each with a training knife and a focus mitt on their left hand which is held across their torso so that it is on the right side of their face. The attacker swing one after the other, as rapidly as possible, with an overhead strike at the defender. They deliver an outside defense to the knife arm and a punch to the attacker (the mitt). Keep the pressure on with rapid attacks. After the person in line attacks they sprint back to the end of the line. This drill can be done with a straight stab or underhand attack as well. The attacks can even be mixed up from one attacker to the next but this slows down the drill a bit.

JOSTLE DRILL: With this drill one person is in the middle being the defender while one partner has a training knife. The rest of the group have targets/shields and all bump, shove and jostle the partner who is the defender. When the partner with the training knife yells "knife" all with targets/shields back off and the partner with the knife attacks. The partner who is defending performs a defense and throws combatives/controls the knife attacker. As soon as this is done the rest of the group go right back to jostling the partner who is defending and the process starts again. We play heavy metal music loudly during this type of drill to add to the stress.

KY DRILL: This is one of the best drills to run and the litmus test for any knife defense. Have both the attacker and defender slather KY jelly or the equivalent on their hands and forearms. This represents blood, which is slippery and almost always present when a knife is involved. This will quickly show what defenses will work and which will not. The practitioner will generally find out that what works the best is blocking, striking and creating distance to get away.

SECOND ATTACKER DRILL: Have the partner who is doing the technique do anything strenuous such as hitting mitts, kneeing a partner who is holding a shield, hitting a heavy bag or even padded up and sparring. The second attacker yells to get the defender's attention and rushes in to stab the defender. The defender pushes off of the first attacker to do the defense. He/she then goes right back to the mitts, shield, etc.

Blunt Object Defenses

"Self defense is a short list of techniques that may get you out alive when you're already screwed"
—SGT Miller

We generally call these stick defenses but they were designed to work against any club/stick type of weapon such as pole cue, tire iron, axe handle, etc. These are certainly used as a distance and impact weapons by the person swinging them. The person being attacked is expected to back up, attempting to get out of range. Bursting into the attacker, who is closing the distance anyway, is a great strategy. Smacking the idiot swinging at you when you get there re sets the loop for the attacker and keeps you from being harmed. Your defense is also offense!

Overhead swing

1) As the attacker rears the stick back to strike they are creating a circle comprised of their head, shoulders and arm. Snap forward at the waist bringing your hands up to your face as if getting ready to dive.

2) Burst off of your right foot (if right handed attacker) and "stab" your left arm to a straight line with your fingers locked and extended (palm facing the attacker's head) through the circle the attacker has created. This will have their

stick/arm slide down your arm and deflect to the side of your body. Simultaneously punch to the face/throat with your right hand.

3) Wrap the attacker's right arm with your left as you put your right palm on the side of the attacker's head and stretch them out. Deliver knees and front kicks to the attacker.

4) When possible stretch the attacker out further and "cup" the end of the stick as you push off of the attacker for the disarm.

 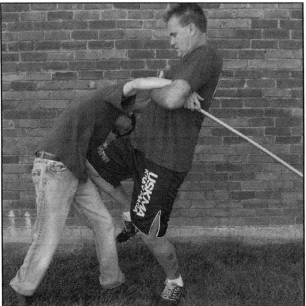

Overhead, off angle

The attacker is coming from a severe angle off of your right side with an overhead swing.

1) Step with your right foot and straighten the right arm as with the overhead stick defense.

2) As the stick is sliding down the outside of your arm pivot step to face the attacker with your forearms up making a wall (in case they follow through and back swing at you).

3) Drop your left hand to their wrist and grab the wrist to control as you punch with your right. Punch several times if needed. Or wrap their arm with yours and throw knees and front kicks, whichever offers itself.

4) For the takeaway simply grab their wrist with one hand and the stick with the other. "Break" their wrist over your knee.

With this defense the blocking arm cannot have any angles or fingers sticking out for the stick to catch. The stick must slide down the back of your hand and down your arm unimpeded. If the attacker is coming with great momentum stab the straight arm out for the stick to slide down and keep travelling in that direction, creating space.

NOTE: If the attacker is closing the distance with a lot of momentum they may simply keep going and create distance after their swing goes down your arm. If you have your own weapon this is the time to draw it. You may also create more distance and run away or close distance and attack before the attacker can get turned around, whichever is called for.

Baseball bat swing

Honestly, when I am teaching blunt object defenses to law enforcement I don't show this technique anymore. Unless someone is going to put a lot of reps into the blunt object defenses they really only need to learn the overhead defense. We found out that, when teaching both at seminars, it was causing hesitation. We would run a drill where the attacker would start from a bit of a distance and it was up to them whether they swung over head or baseball bat. Everyone hesitated for a split second before reacting, trying to decide what attack was coming. We heard ourselves many times say "Well, if you are going to guess wrong guess wrong and do the overhead defense, it'll keep you safer." If we are early/see the attack coming it truly doesn't matter which one we do, we are getting inside of the swinging stick where we won't get hit and can do damage. If we are late and don't see it until the last second guessing wrong when it was a baseball swing gets our ribs broken. If we are late and guess wrong that it's baseball we will get our skull crushed. Just teach to react, burst in with the overhead swing and do damage. If you wish to learn the baseball bat defense:

1) As the (right handed) attacker pulls the stick back to their side collapse on your left side by bending and pointing inward the left knee and rolling your left shoulder forward as you bend forward at the waist. Simultaneously drop your left arm along your left side and bring your right hand to the left side of your face, palm out.

2) Burst off of your right foot at a 45 degree angle so that your body strikes the attacker's arm. Note that you are not bursting towards the attacker's body but towards the wrist which can be three feet to the right of the body.

3) Wrap your left arm around their right and elbow the attacker's face with your right as you straighten your body to stand tall in a "corkscrew" motion.

4) Continue to wrap the attacker's right arm with your left as you put your right palm on the side of the attacker's head and stretch them out to deliver knees and front kicks to the attacker.

5) When possible take your right hand and grab the far end of the stick. Push it down and back in a "U" motion to disarm. Do not turn your back to the attacker to reach for the stick but push your left shoulder forward to bring the stick to your view.

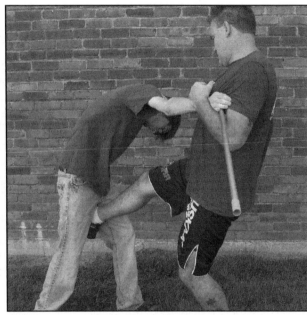

Seminar: Blunt Weapon Defenses (2-hour)

1) Overhead swing defense

2) Line drill; one person after the other swings at defender.

3) 3rd attacker. Hitting heavy bag, scuffling with other student or hitting pads and 3rd person swings at defender

4) Attacker coming from severe right angle

5) Can show baseball bat defense

6) Drill; partner attacks several times mixing up the attacks. Overhead, off angle and baseball bat.

Drills:

SWING DRILL: One partner swings the stick back and forth rapidly. The partner who is defending times the swing to perform the baseball bat defense. The defense can be done on the back swing as well, just left handed.

LINE DRILL: Several 'attackers' with sticks stand in a straight line. They one at a time swing overhead at the partner who is defending one after the other. The partner who is defending does the defense without the combatives, pushes that attacker off and defends the next. The attackers keep sprinting to the back of the line and keep the pressure on. This can also be done with the baseball bat defense.

SECOND ATTACKER DRILL: Have one partner doing anything strenuous such as hitting mitts, kneeing a partner who is holding a shield, hitting a heavy bag or even padded up and sparring. The second attacker yells and bursts in swinging the stick; the defender pushes off of the first attacker and performs the stick defense. He/she then goes right back to the mitts, shield, etc.

5

Handgun

"Instructors, when someone is coming to you to learn self defense they are literally putting their lives in your hands!"
—M. Slane

There are many different thoughts about when to "go" for a weapon disarm. I have had some instructors tell me to act while the gunman is talking, as they are in the loop and must stop talking, realize that you are acting and change what they are doing. I have been told to act when the gunman says "raise your hands" as he/she is expecting hands to move at that point anyway. These make sense in the gym. These are logical and good points. I don't subscribe to either of them. My thought is to always act the split second I realize there is a weapon pointed at me, for several reasons. One is that I don't know if a weapon is being pointed at me with commands such as "give me your money" to follow or if a weapon is being pointed at me and the trigger is being pulled. If a stranger is pointing a deadly weapon at me I must assume the worst…that he/she us firing. Secondly, I know a big adrenaline (and other chemicals) dump is about to hit me. I will have heavy arms, won't be able to judge distances, will shake, will become clumsy, etc. Why would I want to wait on this? I am racing this reaction.

When USKMA instructors teach handgun disarms seminars, whether to citizens or law enforcement, we strive to teach the easiest to learn, easiest to remember and most effective grouping of techniques we possibly can. This is why our "go to" handgun disarm is the Cupping Defense. We prefer this technique over the more popular "pin the gun to the gunman's hip and punch" technique for several reasons. These include:

1) When we have two hours to teach disarms that include a punch we would need most of that time to teach an effective punch. The cupping technique has a kick to the groin, most can do that effectively already.

2) We feel that this technique works better for smaller people. For example, expecting a small female officer to keep a handgun pinned to the hip of a linebacker sized criminal while punching him into submission is asking a lot in our opinion. This defense keeps both of her hands on the weapon with her weight on the handgun as she kicks to the groin.

3) This defense is much easier to be ambidextrous with. If our partner or anyone else that we don't want shot is standing beside us we can redirect the weapon to the opposite side without much difficulty. The other defense forces us to punch left handed if we redirect in the opposite direction, most of us do not have as much power punching with our off hand.

4) Again, we really like having both hands on the weapon. If the defense goes to pot, the weapon is slippery, the gunman is extremely strong, etc. we have a much better chance of keeping the weapon redirected if we have both of our hands controlling it.

5) With the Cupping Defense we can learn one defense that will protect us in five or six different positions/scenarios. This is gold because if we find ourselves with a handgun pointed at us there is nothing to think about, no other defenses to choose from, we can just react. This also cuts way down on practice time as we are learning one defense for six positions that we find ourselves in instead of six different defenses.

Handgun; Cupping From The Front

Whether your hands are up or down (usually up in reality) this first move must be made with no motion except for your hand going to the weapon. No big body motion, foot shuffle, bend at the waist, etc.

1) Take your right hand directly to the weapon in the shortest route possible. You are not grabbing the handgun. If you attempt to grab there is not much room to miss and under this stress we need as much "miss room" as possible. Use an open hand aiming the webbing of the thumb to the trigger guard. This gives you about a seven inch surface to redirect the weapon with. As soon as the weapon is touched redirect it off of your body and then wrap your hand around the barrel to control it. During the redirection keep the handgun on the same plane to ensure the weapon clears your body in a straight line in the shortest route possible. In other words, if the handgun is at neck level when aimed it is still at neck level after it has been redirected. Include a slight body turn at this same time. Do not stay squared up but let your right shoulder turn towards the attacker. This blades your body a bit making your torso a smaller target and gets the

weapon off quicker and also has your momentum falling towards the gunman if the defense fails. You will be in a much better position to attack and control the weapon than if your body was falling away from the gunman.

2) Next, send your left hand to the hammer of the weapon and wrap the hammer as you step in with your left foot to deliver a knee or front kick to the groin with the right leg. As the kicking leg is being placed back to the ground snap the handgun to your waist. Press the right forearm tightly against your stomach and the left forearm against your side as you snap and twist the barrel of the handgun up and towards the attacker.

3) Once his/her grip is broken, pull the handgun away with force. Use your whole body (not just arms) to strike the barrel of the gun to the attackers face or head and back off at an angle looking to escape. If the gunman rushes you before you have created enough distance to access your firearm (if LE or concealed carriers) push off of your back leg and strike to the attacker's face with the barrel using your whole body. For Law Enforcement we teach to keep the handgun that you took away in your off hand as you access and fire (if needed) your personal handgun with your strong hand. We have seen time and time again (in our training) that if the officer accesses their handgun with their two hand grip (like they have done for thousands of rounds in training) when the assailant rushes the officer with a knife he will take stab wounds as he fires his handgun with both hands instead of letting go of his weapon with one hand to block the knife. What we train comes out under stress, we won't come up with a new plan while being attacked.

After spending time learning this defense the next five take very little practice time. They are all the same defense, just different scenarios.

Handgun from right side of head

1) If the handgun is not pressed against your head turn to look at it. It is very difficult to judge distance using peripheral vision. Swipe palm out at the handgun as if swatting a fly buzzing your ear. As you wrap the muzzle snap your head back to get the handgun offline as quickly as possible.

2) Move your off hand to the hammer as you cup. At this same time pivot on your feet to orient towards the assailant. The rest of the defense is identical to the regular cupping defense.

Handgun, defender kneeling

This is the "execution" position.

1) Reach with your strong hand and simultaneously slightly turn your body redirecting the barrel with the webbing of your thumb into the trigger guard.

2) After redirecting the barrel send your other hand to wrap the hammer and simultaneously raise your left knee to get the left foot on the ground, preparing to rise. The cup helps you to have control over the weapon as the assailant will actually help you to stand up as he/she pulls on the handgun.

3) With or without this help spring up on the left foot and send your right leg for a kick to the groin. The rest of the defense is identical to our regular cupping defense.

When we teach this technique to law enforcement officers we talk quite a bit about tactics. If the gunman is too far from me to grab the weapon:

- I will get up and run away. A trained gunman can hardly hit a moving target.

- If I can't run (family with me) I will get up and charge the scumbag with the gun. I may die but I will take him with me and my family will be safe.

- If I am injured and can't really burst up I may try to insult him closer. "Hey pussy, do this like a man…put it between my eyes."

- If I am commanded to cross my ankles and interlock my fingers I will shift my weight and wiggle my elbows. Unless he goes back there to look he won't know that I didn't but it will appear that I did. The scumbags watch "Cops". They know what will make it harder for me to react.

Handgun, defender mounted

This defense is used if you are on the ground with the assailant sitting on your chest pointing the handgun at the head.

1) Redirect the handgun off your body with your right hand and send the left to cup the hammer.

2) Pull sharply down towards the ground a foot to a foot and a half from your head and in line with your eyes as if attempting to bury the muzzle into the ground (with the barrel slightly turned away to protect from ricochets).

3) As you pull burst your hips into a basic ground fighting "buck and roll". Dig your feet into the ground and shoot your hips as hard as possible towards the shoulder that you are rolling the assailant over.

4) As you roll keep weight on the handgun as it should never lose contact with the ground.

5) Finish the roll and end up on top in the "guard" position with the weapon still pushed into the ground.

6) Scrape the muzzle along the ground with great force towards the assailant's hip. By using two hands and body weight on the weapon the handgun will pop out of the attacker's hand fairly easily. If not use the muzzle to strike the assailant and/or take the sight into the attacker's throat and rip it down the torso to the navel. Both of these techniques will give you leverage to pop the handgun out of the attacker's hand.

7) After taking the handgun and striking the attacker with it back off on your knees until sure that you can get up safely. This is important as we have seen defenders jump right to their feet only to become light headed and hit the ground again.

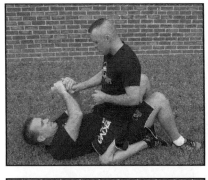

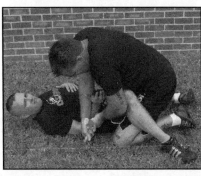

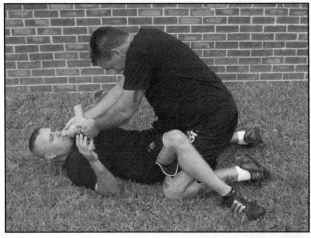
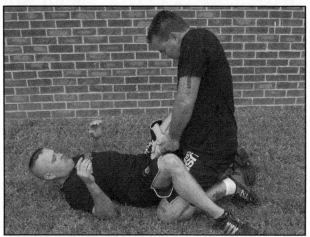

Handgun, gunman in guard

1) Use your right hand to redirect the weapon then send the offhand to wrap and finish the cupping. It is very important to lock the right elbow and keep the right arm straight to prevent the handgun from being turned back on your body.

2) Put your left foot on the assailant's hip and push off to create some distance. If flexibility is an issue place your shin across the gunman's abdomen instead.

3) "Ride the bike with anger" sending stomp kick after stomp kick to the assailant's body and face. The attacker will either let go or be kicked into unconsciousness.

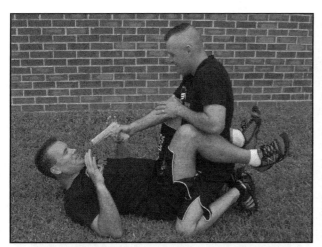

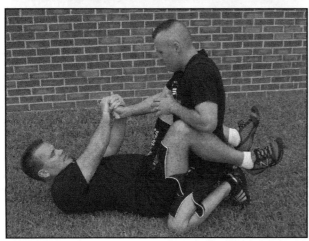
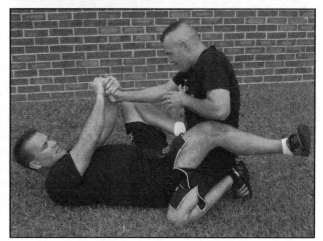

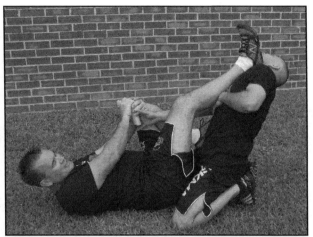

Handgun, gunman standing over

1) Get the handgun offline with your right hand and finish the cupping with the left. As you cup pivot on the ground to get your feet between your head and the assailant. As with the "in the guard" defense keep the right arm straight throughout.

2) "Ride the bike with anger" kicking at the assailants knees, body and face. The only choice he/she has is to get kicked into oblivion, let go or dive on you. Keep your knees up and feet pointed at his/her navel or higher to keep the gunman from diving on top of you.

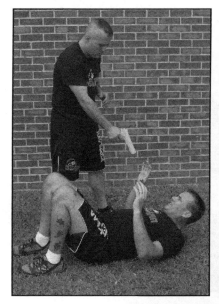
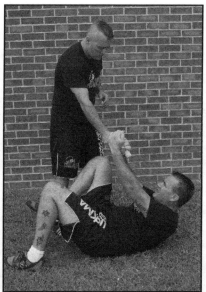
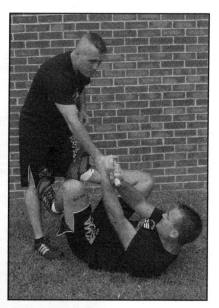

Handgun from across table/counter

1) Perform the cupping defense, brace your foot at the bottom of the counter and sharply pull the gunman towards you.

2) Slam the back of the gunman's hand down on the corner of the table or counter until disarmed.

Be aware that you have done nothing to injure the attacker. They may well jump over the counter to attack you to get their gun back. Use the weapon to strike the barrel to their face and throw combatives.

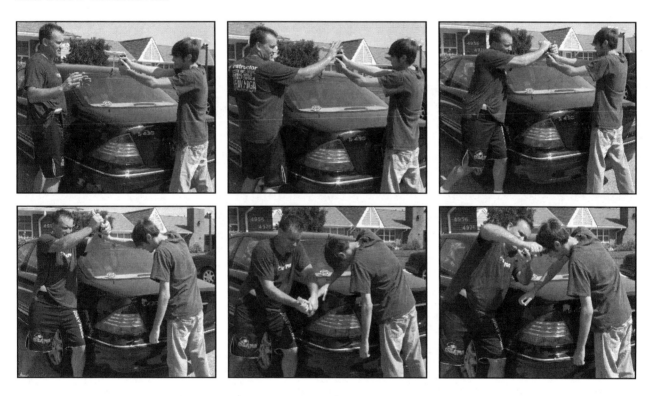

I am asked often "Can't you hurt your hand grabbing the gun like that". Well, I usually think "We tried Jedi mind tricks but they weren't working very well so we decided that we just gotta grab the thing" but I try not to be quite so smart aleck to those paying for a seminar! My patient and kind explanation is "Yep, you can certainly get your hand burned. There are youtube videos of people holding a semi-automatic while it's being fired and they are fine but I know a guy who go cut to the bone doing that. Myth Busters has shown that a revolver's gas discharge can actually blow a finger off but you won't know it until after the event and the adrenaline starts to wear off. I didn't say we would come out of this situation unscathed. We are in a world of crap and have a list of crappy answers. At the bottom of the crappy answer list is to stand there and get shot. At the top of the list is our defense. The only good answer is to not be there with a handgun pointed at you in the first place!" I've even been asked about keeping the handgun by our head as we take it off...the person was afraid of being deafened. Sigh...I am not teaching magic tricks and, again, I didn't say you'd be unscathed!

You will also be asked, by someone standing fifteen feet away, "What is your defense from here?" I had an Israeli instructor once who was asked that and he replied "I'm not f@$%ing God...I have to be able to touch the God D#$%$d thing!!" Good answer. If I am so far away that I can't touch the weapon I will run. A trained gunman can hardly hit a moving target. If a bullet hits a place that will kill me in that scenario it was my day to die...God knew that centuries ago! Now if I can't run...see the paragraph after the "kneeling" handgun defense.

Gun from behind

1) As you feel the handgun in your back look over your left shoulder at the gunman's off hand (1). You can assume that it is a handgun in your back but must make sure the weapon isn't in the attacker's off hand.

2) When you see that the off hand is clear continue to turn your torso swatting with your palm out across your rear end (as if swatting a sniffing dog).

3) After redirecting the handgun burst off of your right foot as you turn and deliver a right elbow to the gunman's face. Your left arm is straight and extending beyond the gunman between his elbow and arm pit, under his arm.

4) Then "curl" your left arm to warp around the assailant's arm that is holding the gun.

5) At the same time you curl use your right palm to stretch out the assailant, pushing the side of their head away. The attacker's gun arm will slide through your wrapped arm until it gets to the wrist. Punch your left shoulder forward to bend his/her hand backwards to make it more difficult to rip the handgun out of your grip.

6) Deliver knees and front kicks.

7) Take away the handgun by grabbing it with your pinky up towards the sky. Wrap the hand around the barrel and snap the barrel back against his/her arm with force. Then slide the handgun forward off of the broken finger, push off, throw a combative if it's there and disengage at an angle drawing your own weapon if you are armed.

Remember that the feet do not move until the burst, the torso turn does the redirection. Do not, while bursting, allow the student to allow their left arm to be between the wrist and elbow of the gunman as when he pulls back the handgun will come out of the attempted wrap. Deliver combatives until the gunman is out and has dropped the handgun, the disarm is only important if the handgun is needed quickly, i.e.: another attacker is closing on you.

Side of head, towards back of head

This is handgun from behind. If the handgun is pointed at the back of the head or the side of the head but towards the back simply do the same defense but "roll" your head around the barrel of the gun as you turn your torso.

Side, behind arm

This is the exact same defense as handgun from behind. It is actually easier because you are already half way turned to deliver the burst and elbow.

 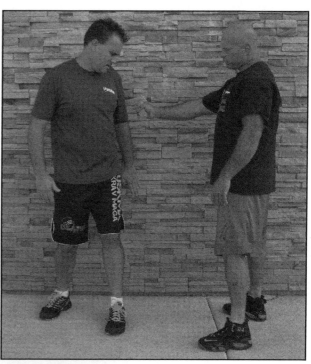

Behind, walking

Nothing changes but the timing. Time this out so that you are stepping with your right foot forward so that you are able to turn and burst correctly.

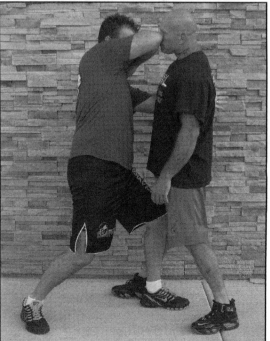

Gun from behind at a distance

As you look over your right shoulder you must locate the handgun, seeing how far away it is and at what level it is being held.

1) Snap forward by bowing at the waist and shoot your right elbow straight back to point at the weapon. Extend your arm to the weapon, redirecting it with your hand.

2) Wrap your hand around the weapon to control it and burst off of your left foot as you turn towards the gunman.

3) Wrap the gunman's wrist with your left hand so that you now have your right hand wrapped around the handgun and the left around the wrist with the handgun pressed against the gunman's body.

4) Throw several combatives including knees to the groin and head butts.

5) Pull the handgun off of the gunman's body and push both of your hands together so that the handgun snaps against the gunman's arm. Do this with your body weight and not just arms (think of a pec deck exercise machine). After this takeaway strike the attacker and create distance.

Gun from behind at a distance, turning left

1) If you turned left you will go to the handgun with your left hand as above and burst off of your right foot as you turn. This is the same defense except the handgun isn't against the gunman's body but off to the side.

2) Keep both hands on the weapon and wrist as you attempt to keep the handgun tight to the side of the gunman and not let it get pushed out in front of the attacker. A punch may also be thrown to the face/throat before the second hand goes to the wrist.

3) The ending is the same as above, throw combatives and "break" the handgun from the attacker's grip.

This is a higher risk disarm as the gun is at a distance that may be difficult to judge. The redirecting arm extends straight from your body and doesn't go to the handgun from the side (no rotation). This pointing of the elbow and snap with the hand will allow you to redirect the weapon even if the distance was misjudged (redirection can be with forearm instead of hand).

Gun from behind, shoulder held; handgun takedown

This defense is the basic "machine gun takedown" that most Krav Maga systems still use for long gun. We have taken this defense out but keep it as a handgun defense for this situation. The gunman has the handgun tucked on their right hip (assuming a right handed gunman) and is walking you with his left hand on your right shoulder to keep you from turning in to the gun.

1) Pivot sharply away from the gunman, towards his/her back as you burst off of your left (pivot) foot towards the gunman's back. As you get to the gunman's back you want to be facing his/her back with your feet pointed in the same direction as his/hers.

2) When you get to the back your left arm has reached under the gunman's gun arm and is pinning it against his/her body as your right arm is shoved as far between the gunman's legs and as tight to the groin as possible. They are basically sitting on your bicep.

3) Do not attempt to lift the gunman off of the ground as they may be much larger than you are. Instead, stand to get them up on their toes and then "pour" them as if they were a heavy bag of flour. As they lose their balance and fall keep pressed up against their back and fall on top of them.

4) Stay mounted on their back and strike to the back of the head with elbows and punches.

You should not attempt to lift the attacker off of the ground as they may be much heavier than you are. Instead, attempt to get them up on their toes and then dump them. Also, as they fall don't let them hit the ground as you are still standing, they will roll and put the handgun back on you. Stay tight and on top of them allowing no distance as they fall and land on top of them.

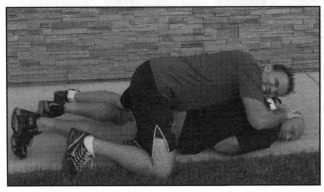

Gun from front, shoulder held; handgun takedown

Same situation as above but the gunman is facing you. He has his left hand extended to your left shoulder (or is pushing/punching your left shoulder) to keep you from pivoting towards the gun.

1) Take your right hand and cup the attacker's left elbow, fingers pointing up. Pull the elbow towards and past you and use this pull to "launch" yourself to the gunman's back. NOTE: if the attacker is punching/popping the shoulder instead of holding it this same technique is used, time the punch and cup the elbow the same way.

2) As you get to the gunman's back be facing his/her back with your feet pointed in the same direction as his/hers.

3) When you get to the back your left arm reaches under the gunman's gun arm and pins it against his/her body as your right arm is shoved as far between the gunman's legs and as tight to the groin as possible. They will basically be sitting on your bicep.

4) Stand to get them up on their toes and then "pour" them as if they were an eighty pound bag of flour. As they lose their balance and fall keep pressed up against their back and fall on top of them.

5) Stay mounted on their back and strike to the back of the head with elbows and punches.

Gun from front, shoulder held or punched

If the handgun is reachable simply ignore the gunman's off hand and do the cupping defense. If the gun is being held further back as the gunman grabs your shoulder/clothing or punches at you to move still do the cupping defense with the following differences.

1) Start the cupping defense but redirect with your left hand, pushing the handgun to your right. At the same time use your right hand to "windshield wiper" the gunman's off hand. Hit the off hand at the wrist sharply.

2) After the hand is redirected continue to move your right hand to the hammer of the weapon.

3) Continue with cupping defense as you kick/knee the gunman,

4) Bring forearms to stomach and hip to take handgun away,

5) Strike attacker with barrel of gun and create distance.

Gun from side, in front of arm

This is one of the few weapon defenses that do not follow the RCAT (redirect, control, attack, takeaway). The takeaway is followed by the attack.

1) Assuming a right handed gunman has the weapon pressed to your left side cup at the butt of the wrist with your left hand palm up with thumb over the wrist.

2) Simultaneously step with your left foot into a "sumo" stance. Make sure the wrist is grabbed and not above the wrist as above the wrist on the forearm will allow the wrist to bend and keep the handgun on you longer. Grabbing the wrist so that it can't bend gets the weapon off your side and directly in front of your body.

3) Grab the barrel with your right hand, palm up, and thumb wrapped over the barrel.

4) With your right elbow on your hip pivot on your right foot towards the attacker so that your body (not just arms) snaps the handgun to the attacker's arm. This disarms the attacker.

5) Take the weapon and strike the barrel into the attacker's face. Retreat at an angle.

Gun From Front, Pushing Into Stomach

If the weapon is touching your stomach simply do the gun from the front defense. If the handgun is pushing hard into your stomach it cannot be redirected properly with that defense. Instead, pivot on our left foot back into a "sumo" stance as you grab the wrist with your left hand and proceed with the previous defense.

Gun from behind, hostage

1) The assailant has his left arm wrapped around you from behind with the right holding a handgun to your head. You can raise our hands and "pat" his arm reassuringly as a ruse to get your hands close to the handgun or simply go straight for the handgun as the gunman (unless he/she is very tall) can't see your hands anyway. Take your right hand and reach over the gun, hooking the barrel and pulling it forward.

2) After clearing your head turn your palm from towards your face to away from your face rapidly to get the barrel pointing form across your body to away from your body, out to the side. As you turn the barrel away snap the handgun directly back towards the gunman almost touching your ear with the hammer to break his/her grip.

3) Place your off hand on the hammer and push with both hands away as sharply as possible. Bend at the waist and snap forward as if diving into a pool, stretching the gunman out.

4) This will probably propel you away from the gunman to create distance. As you are creating this distance you can try to throw an elbow back to the gunman's head and even kick off if necessary. Create distance to tap and rack or access your own weapon.

It is important when pushing out to really pop the hips back and stretch out as far as possible. You should look like you are diving into water when doing this part of the defense.

Hostage pinned against wall

This scenario is being pinned face first into a wall. The gunman has the barrel of the weapon on the back of your head as you are being pushed in to a wall. This is identical to the defense above but you do not have the room to push the gun forward and stretch the gunman out. "Cup" the handgun and get it in front of you then snap it back with the barrel pointed away from you as above but instead of stretching the gunman out trap the handgun against the wall with both hands and throw combatives at the gunman.

Handgun, mounted on back

1) Reach with your right hand to the barrel and sharply pull the handgun down to the ground in front of your right shoulder. Pin the handgun to the ground by also grabbing the gunman's wrist with your left hand.

2) At the same time bend your knee to get your foot up under your body to push off of. Push off of your left foot and "toe pick" the gunman's arm. You aren't pushing up but pushing your body along the ground. The arm will break or the gunman will fall forward and onto the ground.

3) Scramble to deliver combatives including knees, head butts and striking the gunman with their own weapon to the face and head (note; keep both hands on the handgun, this will give you leverage and strength over his/her one hand on the weapon).

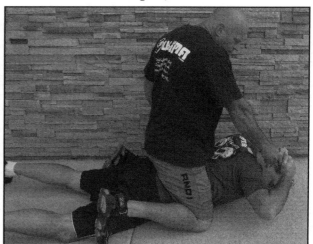
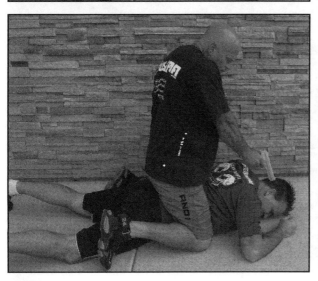
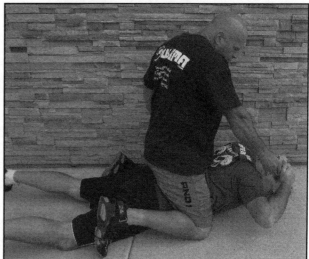

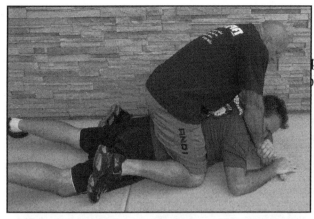

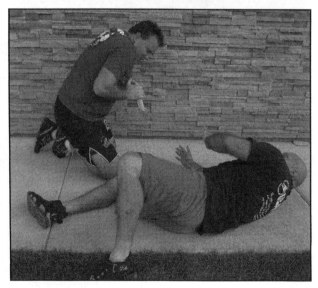

Hostage from behind, gun to side of body

1) Turn sharply to your right allowing your arm to pin the handgun against the gunman's body.

2) Turn into the gunman and catch the gunman's elbow with your left hand (assuming a right handed attacker). Continue the turn keeping the handgun in the crook of your right arm's elbow. Hug the gunman tight while holding the elbow so the gunman can't pull the gun out. You are squeezing the arm holding the gun between your bodies as you grab high on the gunman's back with your right arm to keep the handgun in the gunman's arm pit.

3) Throw knees and head butts at the gunman while holding tight. To take away pivot step away from the gun while hooking his wrist with your right forearm and pushing on his elbow with your left palm. Throw more combatives from here as you reach the left hand to the handgun for the takeaway.

4) You can also end this with a takedown forcing the attacker's face into the ground. Slide your body into the attacker's arm pit, raise your left leg and sit down. Keep control of the handgun as you do this and, once you are on the ground, throw elbows to the attacker's head or draw your own weapon for a contact shot.

Hostage from behind, on knees

This is a high risk defense, even more so if the gunman is at a distance.

1) Reach back to grab the handgun and, after grabbing, continue to turn to elbow and punch the attacker low line.

2) Another option (if gun is closer/touching your head) is to pull the handgun in front of you and push it to the floor with both hands. As you take the handgun to the ground base out on it and throw a back kick to the knees or midsection (or even face if they are following the handgun down). Throw combatives until you have the handgun and can get to your feet.

Teaching A Handgun Seminar

I have taught a lot of handgun disarm seminars over the years. Our "Cupping Handgun Defenses Seminar" is about a two to two and a half hour seminar. The layout for this seminar is as follows:

Seminar: Handgun Disarms (2 to 2 ½ hours)

1) Show cupping defense to handgun from the front. Work on this for a while and get it down because all the rest are a piece of cake after learning this one.

   Once it looks good, have them practice with a little more realism:

   - At different levels and ranges, gunman holding with one hand or two, etc., as soon as gun is raised, etc.

   - With gunman acting realistic....cussing, yelling, pushing, slapping.

2) "Pummel drill" Everyone is hitting/pushing the person who is "it" in the middle with shields...the student with the gun yells "gun" and everyone gets out of the way. The person who is in the middle does the defense. Do four quick reps and the next person it "it".

   - Once cupping from the front looks good and they've had a chance to practice it under some stress, teach additional defenses that build off of that basic technique:

3) Cupping from the right side of head

4) From kneeling

5) From mount

6) From guard

7) Gunman standing over

8) Reintroduce the pummel drill but now the gunman is at a distance and commands the defender to get to their knees or lay on their back then the gunman gets into the guard, mount or stands over.

The teaching points we make during this seminar:

- Never hand the gun back and forth. Drop it on the ground each time you wish to give it back to your partner. What we do in training comes out of us under stress. I have heard several stories (one from Lt. Col Grosman's book On Killing) of police officers practicing disarms and handing the gun right back to their partner only to do a disarm on the street and hand it right back to the bad guy!

- Hands are faster than body, body is faster than feet. If you are stepping you are making it as slow as you possibly can. The hand goes straight to the weapon, do not hitch your body, step or anything else until the weapon is redirected!

- When asked "where should I look, at the gun or at them?" I always answer "I can't tell you where, under the stress of 'I'm about to die' you will look. Cops will tell you that a person who has had a gun in their face can either describe the gun to a t but don't know what the person looked like or they can describe the person very well but don't know what the gun looked like. When you start the defense it probably helps to look at what you are trying to redirect."

- We cannot assume this snap to our waist will take the handgun away (although, honestly, it almost always does if done correctly). If it doesn't come out of the gunman's hand we still have two hands on the weapon to his/her one. Go forward with rage, take the handgun with their hand still on it and beat their head in with that hunk of metal they gave you!

- The scumbag will rush you to get their gun back. You think you're just going to shoot them? Do you know where the safety release is on a Bersa .380, a Colt 45, a Glock 19? Do you know how to fix the jam I can almost guarantee you that you just created? Do you know if the idiot had it loaded with the right ammo or loaded at all? As you are pressing a trigger that doesn't work and stuck in that loop the scumbag will get to you and start attacking. Don't think "shoot", think "Push off of my back foot and see how far I can jam this barrel into their skull as they get closer."

- When learning these defenses it is not uncommon for me to see students stopping in mid take away and starting over because they messed up. This is a major no no! I tell them that under stress they will react when it's real exactly how they trained. There aren't a lot of bad guys who are going to let them stop and start over...this will get them shot for sure! So we don't do it when training! If they mess up they need to continue. After all, Krav isnt' about the technique (those fall apart under stress and exhaustion), it is about the philosophy of get the weapon pointed offline and beat the attacker into the ground. I tell them to make it up and win...if i like what they did I'll teach it that way and name it after them!

- If you have your own weapon, of course you want to access that as you are creating distance. Do not throw the other weapon down or put it in your arm pit or belt. The problem is, under this stress and adrenaline, your training on shooting will take over. Most of us have practiced shooting two handed. As the scumbag pulls a knife and rushes you you will keep both hands on your gun as you fire, taking stab wounds as you do. You will not come up with the plan of "let go of the weapon with one hand and block as I shoot". We recommend keeping the scumbag's weapon in your off hand and draw your weapon with your strong hand. Holding his/her weapon in that off hand will force you to fire one handed and the probability of blocking with the off hand is greatly increased.

- Explain that when the gun is dropped not to dive for the gun. If the gun hits the ground invariably both the "bad guy" and the Kravist will both dive for the weapon. This gives us only a 50/50 chance of winning. Teach that while the assailant is thinking "go for the gun" we should again be thinking "hurt the bad guy". As the assailant is diving for the gun, knee them in the face. We know the space they are about to be in, attack it! Use combatives to put them down and then you have plenty of time to walk over and pick up the rifle/shotgun.

Drills

The main thing to remember as instructors is that to teach only technique is a SIN! To save a life (your own or someone else's) the technique is maybe 40% of what the student needs. How many dash cam or surveillance videos have you seen where the officer or security guard in the fight is doing anything that even remotely resembles his/her training? I would guess not very often. It is almost as if we survive in spite of our training, not because of it. Much more important than the techniques that are taught is the attitude and philosophy that is being taught. The attitude must be "I am going home today no matter what." We must teach aggression, a fighting "never say die" spirit and put all training into realistic scenarios. We cannot just teach techniques as an end all but must practice the techniques under stress, while exhausted and under realistic circumstances. If we train a handgun disarm, for example, always with the partner standing like a statue with the handgun pointed at us it is an entirely different feeling on the street when the attacker is punching us with the gun, slapping us, cussing and screaming. If we had never had an attacker come at us like this in training we haven't trained for it, we won't have a plan and it will not come out of us. If we train properly we will have the "been there, done that" feeling that we need to stay safe.

Realism Drill: This is not really a drill but the way to train each technique. Simply have the gunman play act and be the criminal. He may cuss, waive the gun, slap, kick and push the officer who is doing the defense (1). The officer defending will do the technique as soon as the gun is presented where he can grab it (2). This can be taken a step further as both the gunman and the defender pad up with mouth piece, headgear, shin pads, etc. as the gunman is now striking, pushing and moving the defender with force. Doing techniques with a partner who is standing like a statue pointing the handgun at us is not what we will see on the streets. This play acting is essential.

Jostle Drill: With this drill one officer is in the middle being the defender while one officer has a training handgun. The rest of the group have targets/shields and all bump, shove and jostle the officer who is defending. When the officer with the training gun yells "gun" all with targets/shields back off and the officer with the gun points it at the officer who is defending. The officer who was defending does the cupping defense, takes the handgun and tosses it to the ground. As soon as this is done the rest of the group go right back to jostling the officer who is it and the process starts again. We play heavy metal music loudly during this type of drill to add to the stress.

The next step of this drill will have the same thing being done but the officer with the handgun will yell "gun" while several feet away. He then gives commands to the officer who is defending to get on their knees, lay on the ground, etc. The officer defending will then do the appropriate defense (cupping from the front, cupping from the knees, cupping mounted, cupping from the guard, cupping standing over, etc.).

Gauntlet Drill: The officer who is defending walks through doorways, around corners, etc. while the attackers are hidden. As soon as the officer sees a handgun presented he/she does the appropriate defense.

Second attacker Drill: Have the officer doing anything strenuous such as hitting mitts, kneeing a partner who is holding a shield, hitting a heavy bag or even padded up and sparring (1). The second attacker yells to get the defender's attention and points the handgun at the defender (2). The officer pushes off of the first attacker to do the defense. He/she then goes right back to the mitts, shield, etc.

Handgun Retention

"Don't hit at all if it is honorably possible to avoid hitting; but never hit softly." Teddy Roosevelt

All of our defense revolve around redirecting and grabbing the handgun. It only makes sense to train for when someone attempts to do this to our weapon. We cover holster grabs for our law enforcement readers and open carry proponents followed by our weapon being out and grabbed.

Handgun retention, holster grab from front

These techniques are identical whether an attacker grabs the holster with one hand or two.

1) As the attacker grabs the weapon in your holster bend forward and bear hug their arms tightly to your chest.

2) Lift up on their arms sharply and deliver front kicks and knees to the attacker's groin.

3) Twist your torso violently from side to side while bear hugging arms to tear the attacker's elbow and shoulder ligaments and tendons.

4) Push off, create distance and draw.

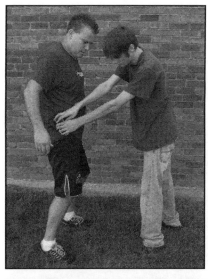

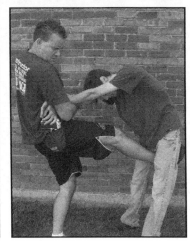

Handgun retention, holster grab from front on knees

If you are grounded on one knee or two and an attacker grabs your holster this technique is virtually identical to the one above.

1) As the attacker grabs your holster put one foot on the ground and stand.

2) Burst up sharply and deliver a front kick to the groin.

3) Twist your torso violently from side to side while bear hugging arms to tear the attacker's elbow and shoulder ligaments and tendons.

4) Push off, create distance and draw.

Handgun retention, holster grab from rear

1) As the attacker grabs your holster from behind use your opposite hand to grab the attacker's wrist to keep it in place.

2) Throw rear elbows to the attacker's head until the attacker let's go. As we have his/her hand we do not even need to look, the head is at the end of the arm you are holding.

3) Push off, create distance and draw.

If the attacker grabs your holster from the side use this same technique by throwing side elbows.

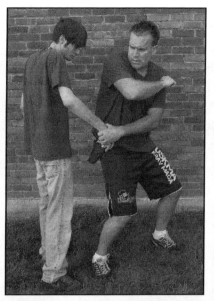
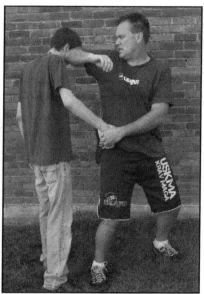

Handgun retention, handgun grab from front

1) As the attacker grabs the handgun burst towards the attacker and simultaneously pull your handgun back toward you. Wrap your other arm around your gun hand and keep the handgun tightly into your body. The trigger guard and grip are in the crook of your arm. The attacker cannot pull the handgun loose as it would have to go through your arm.

2) Sharply lift up and strike with knees and front kicks to the groin.

3) Push off, create distance and draw.

Handgun retention, handgun grab from side

1) As the attacker grabs the handgun pivot towards the attacker and burst towards them as you simultaneously pull the handgun back toward you. Wrap your other arm around your gun hand and keep the handgun tightly into your body. The trigger guard and grip are in the crook of your arm. The attacker cannot pull the handgun loose as it would have to go through your arm.

2) Sharply lift up and strike with knees and front kicks to the groin.

3) Push off, create distance and draw.

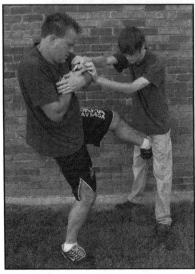

Handgun retention, handgun grab from front, supine

This is a position that you generally wouldn't find yourself in but it's possible that you tripped or were knocked to the ground.

1) From the ground as the attacker grabs your pistol use his pulling force to assist you in rising as you keep a tight grip on the weapon.

2) As you stand burst towards the attacker and simultaneously pull your handgun back toward you. Wrap your other arm around your gun hand and keep the handgun tightly into your body. The trigger guard and grip are in the crook of your arm. The attacker cannot pull the handgun loose as it would have to go through your arm.

3) Sharply lift up and strike with knees and front kicks to the groin.

4) Push off, create distance and draw.

Notes:

- Avoid being in a tug of war. Advance on the attacker as you pull the weapon into your body.

- If in a deadly force situation pulling the trigger when the attacker is in front of the barrel is good strategy. Make sure the barrel is outside of your arm at all times, the trigger guard and handle is what is caught in the crook of your arm.

Handgun retention, handgun grab from behind

This is when your arms are extended and the attacker reaches for your pistol over or around your shoulders.

1) Sharply pull the handgun back in toward your core with the barrel pointed down and away.

2) Pivot your hips so that your handgun is away from the attacker.

3) With your free arm strike the attacker in the stomach and sternum with elbows to create some space.

4) Create distance and face the attacker with handgun aimed at the attacker.

7

3rd party

There is a time when we need to intervene! Too many people are afraid to help anyone. They won't risk anything, even to save a life. They realize that it is dangerous to help others, and they prefer to live a life in fear rather than having principles, things that they won't put up with. Even worse are the people who won't help because they may be liable. These people would watch someone be beaten to death rather than take a chance of being sued or going to jail. What happened to caring and watching out for each other? Wow.

There are things worth risking life and limb for. It seems that most of America doesn't want to risk anything for anyone. In SGT Strong's book STRONG ON DEFENSE he talks about a woman who was abducted and tortured for weeks. She escaped once from the scumbag's car on a highway as she was being moved. She ran down the highway and he chased her, grabbed her by the hair and pulled her back to the car. Not only did nobody stop to help, nobody even called the police! There are times to intervene…but it is dangerous to do so. I'm not talking about standing up for a lady's honor in a bar because some biker slapped her on the rear. You aren't the protector of the world. However, if someone is being seriously injured, even if a stranger, it is probably time to jump in.

When you do have to intervene, there are things to keep in mind.

1) Just like with self protection when it is go time you go with all you have. You go extreme and you go ballistic. If you think that your response may be too extreme you shouldn't be intervening. Keep the pressure on and go until you and whoever you are helping are safe. This is usually when the scumbag is knocked unconscious! We aren't looking to restrain or put in a "come along" type of joint lock. If that is all that needs done nobody was in very much danger. What are you going to do after you have them in a joint lock….walk them to the courthouse? What do you do when his buddy shows up, let go and have two to worry about? Unless you are law enforcement, a bouncer or a school

teacher don't "control" with a joint lock! Do major damage with the goal being to get the heck out of there.

2) Keep the attacker in sight but don't have tunnel vision. It makes sense not to take your eyes off of the threat. Watch his hands, are they going to his pocket for a weapon (keep in mind that every scumbag carries at least a blade)? Is he heading for the pool cues? Does he appear to know how to fight? Although you have to watch him you can't have tunnel vision and see only him. Everyone, even scumbags, have buddies. When you jump in they will jump you. Again, go hard with the goal being to get yourself and the victim out of there.

3) Be safe. Anything goes. If you are in a fight to save a life (and it's yours that you are trying to save as well when you insert yourself into the problem) anything goes. If the situation calls for it hit them with the car you are driving. Pick up a brick. Use whatever you can get your hands on. Again, if you think what you are doing may be too extreme, the situation wasn't bad enough to put yourself into.

When you have no choice but to put yourself into a bad situation to save another; be smart about it. Look at the threat as targets. If you look only at targets it doesn't matter how big they are, how mean they look or even what they are doing to you. You see targets that need hit…and hit them as hard as you can. Remember to constantly be looking to disengage and get yourself and the person you are helping to safety.

3rd party knife

If the knife is off of the attacker (pointed but not touching) you simply burst in and wrap the attacker's knife holding arm and throw combatives as in the overhead, underhand and straight attack. If the attacker is behind the victim holding them tight and the blade is at the victim's throat:

1) If coming from the right side (assuming a right handed attacker) strike/push on the elbow to push knife off of victim's throat.

2) Wrap the knife wielding arm with both of your arms

3) Throw combatives

4) Wrap the attacking arm and throw combatives until the attacker is unconscious or you can push off and get away. If a takeaway is needed curl your left arm to bring the knife in front of you and then put your right hand's fingers over their fingers and take away with a cavalier (pulling the wrist with your left hand as you push with your right, bending their hand behind their arm in a direction that it doesn't want to go).

If coming from the left side:

1) This isn't optimal but about the only thing to do is shove both open hands behind the knife/wrist/forearm. Getting your hands between the blade and the victim's throat.

2) Pull the knife arm away and wrap the arm with both of yours.

3) Throw combatives.

4) Wrap the attacking arm and throw combatives until the attacker is unconscious or you can push off and get away. If a takeaway is needed curl your left arm to bring the knife in front of you and then put your right hand's fingers over their fingers and take away with a cavalier (pulling the wrist with your left hand as you push with your right, bending their hand behind their arm in a direction that it doesn't want to go).

A knife defense that grabs the blade is a poor choice. The only defense for this attack and the angle you arrive at is the above. There are situations we certainly don't want to be in but, if we are, the choice has to be made.

3rd Party Handgun

Beside victim – facing gunman

1) Burst to the gun with both palms in front of your body (whether fingers are pointed up or down depends on height the weapon is being held).

2) One hand grabs the wrist while the other grabs the gun's barrel (make sure that the hand grabbing the barrel is the first one to arrive, if you hit the wrist first the wrist will bend keeping the gun on the victim).

3) Pivot on your left foot (if coming from the gunman's right) to use your body as you snap the handgun to the gunman's forearm.

4) Pull the handgun away from the attacker and strike the attacker in the face with the barrel using full body/torso turn rather than just your arm.

5) Lead victim away as you create distance or strike the gunman with combatives until no longer a threat.

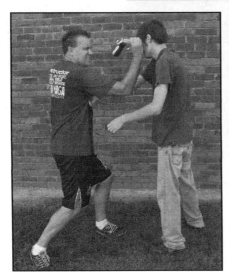

Beside victim facing away from gunman and/or victim being walked

1) Burst with both palms in front of your body (whether fingers are pointed up or down depends on height the weapon is being held).

2) One hand grabs the wrist while the other grabs the gun's barrel (make sure that the hand grabbing the barrel is the first one to arrive, if you hit the wrist first the wrist will bend keeping the gun on the victim).

3) Pivot on your left foot (if coming from the gunman's right) to use your body as you snap the handgun to the gunman's forearm.

4) Pull the handgun away from the attacker and strike the attacker in the face with the barrel using full body/torso turn rather than just your arm (if victim is close enough push them with your elbow as you bring arm back to throw this strike).

5) Lead victim away as you create distance or strike the gunman with combatives until no longer a threat.

Behind victim

1) As you approach sprint to left side of victim.

2) Try to time it so that your right foot lands beside the victims left foot as you hook your right hand over the victims left shoulder and "launch" yourself through the air to the gunman.

3) Reach out with your left hand to grab and redirect the barrel of the gun. Land and strike the gunman with right hand as you keep handgun pinned to gunman's right hip with your left hand.

4) Take right hand to hammer of the weapon and twist it violently out of gunman's hand.

5) Strike the gunman with the barrel of the handgun as you back out. Lead victim away as you create distance or strike the gunman with combatives until no longer a threat.

This is a high risk disarm as the gunman can see your approach. This is designed to get us to the gun as quickly as possible. One thing to keep in mind is that the gunman is under the same stress as we are and may well have tunnel vision on the victim and not notice that you are there until the handgun is actually redirected. Use violence of motion and be quick once you decide that it's go time!

Behind gunman

1) Stay in line with gunman and victim as you approach gunman to keep from being seen. Stay crouched as you approach gunman to stay out of his/her peripheral vision.

2) As you approach gunman try to time it so that your left foot lands directly beside the gunman's right (assuming a right handed gunman). Pivot on your left foot to get right hand on barrel and redirect. Again, whether palms have fingers pointed up or down depends on the height the gun is being held.

3) Grab the gunman's wrist with your left hand and continue to pivot to place yourself between the gunman and the victim as you end up face to face with the gunman. Use your body as you snap the handgun to the gunman's forearm.

4) Pull the handgun away from the attacker and strike the attacker in the face with the barrel using full body/torso turn rather than just your arm (if victim is close enough push them with your elbow as you bring arm back to throw this strike).

5) Lead victim away as you create distance or strike the gunman with combatives until no longer a threat.

Victim in choke/hostage

1) Burst to the gunman's forearm with both hands, fingers pointed up. You will be on the victim's right side if it is a right handed gunman. Have your right hand hit the barrel and redirect it before your left hand grabs the gunman's wrist (if you grab the wrist first the wrist will bend and the barrel will remain on the victim).

2) Explosively ram the barrel of the gun into the gunman's face or clavicle.

3) Push the barrel into the pressure point of the clavicle straight down to drop the gunman or, keeping both hands on the handgun and attacker's wrist, strike the gun barrel to the gunman's face over and over until the gunman is finished.

4) Lead victim away as you create distance or strike the gunman with combatives until no longer a threat.

A bit more on intervening. Having a plan for any situation will get us moving. Under stress our head goes to "mid brain" and we won't be able to come up with a plan. If we planned ahead of time the plan will surface and we will act. Having "go buttons" is a form of mind setting.

Go buttons are thinking beforehand about what you will not tolerate. If, for example, I see a woman being slapped by a man out in public and never thought about what I would do in that situation I will hesitate, go off half-heartedly or even put myself in unnecessary danger. If I had thought about it before hand I will act with the plan that is already in my head.

Now, go buttons aren't a "Samurai Code" of ethics or a "Hero Philosophy". They are just things that you have stated to yourself that you will not let happen in your presence. This hero stuff or "Savior of the World" code is something we leave for the martial arts, we don't teach these things. The scum bags don't have codes or "Never strike first" philosophies so to teach these to our students automatically puts them behind the eight ball. If the scum bags are going to use violence as a weapon we must perfect violence and wield it better than they do.

It's a good idea to write down your "go buttons". To think about them and to have a plan. Here are some of mine:

- I will not allow a woman to be hit in my presence. Yes, I understand the dynamics of spousal abuse. I may get jumped by him and her both but this is something I will not walk by and ignore.

- I will not allow a child to be hit in my presence. I believe in a good spanking when deserved but I will intervene if an adult is slapping down a child or otherwise hitting a child inappropriately.

- If a child says that someone grabbing them is not their parent I will intervene. Most of us would I would hope.

- If two dudes are squaring off and fighting…oh well, have fun. If one is unconscious and the other is still beating them I will intervene up to a point. IF they are both gang bangers and the rest of the group is standing around this would be suicide. I think of these things in advance however.

- If a store, bank, business is being robbed…oh well, they are insured. I am not the savior of the universe!

- If someone threatens my friends or family I will come out swinging. There will be no words or puffing up…there will be fists.

- If someone keeps approaching me and I have told them to stop I will hit them when they are close enough. They have ignored warnings and I will not wait to see if they really mean business.

- If I see a police officer in a fight and he/she isn't obviously winning I will jump in and help him or her.

- If any stranger is in my house there will be no questions, there will be great bodily harm.

- I will never be bound. I will fight three dudes with guns now even with those very thin odds than be at their mercy later.

- I will never be moved to another spot or allow anyone else to be moved. The secondary crime scene is where the scum bag has solitude and time.

- I will not stop my car because someone is blocking it with another vehicle or even their body. I am in a 3,400 pound weapon and I will use it.

So what are your go buttons? Think about them before hand and have a plan.

Car Jacking

"Danger, if met head on, can be nearly halved"
—W. Churchill

We generally think of carjacking being attempted using a handgun. This will be the majority of the defenses that we cover but they can certainly bring a knife, long gun or any other weapon to the game.

If someone wants your car, get out and let them have it. There is no reason to fight for something that insurance will replace. There are certainly times that you must fight. If your family is in the car I am sure you aren't getting out and letting them drive off with them. I actually knew a person who was "carjacked"…he was getting out of his car and was shot in the head before he even knew another person was close. With this in mind, I am probably fighting every time. Letting the scumbag have my car is no guarantee that he doesn't attempt to murder me.

First off, when driving in a city keep your doors locked and your windows up. This takes care of you being the easy carjacking. The scumbag may well pass you up and look for the idiot with the windows down, doors unlocked and texting at the stop light. If approached, step on the gas and get out of there.

A blog I wrote years ago about being in a car:

We at the USKMA strive to teach safety and self defense for the real world. In the real world we spend a lot of time in a car. What can we do to be safe in our car? Read on!

We teach some way cool carjacking techniques for handgun disarms while seated in a car. We use the door frame, steering wheel, etc. to beat the bad guys hand against or to use for leverage. When we are teaching self defense in class we teach 1) don't be there, 2) run, 3) pick up something to use as a weapon and 4) self defense techniques. The actual laying on of hands for self defense comes last. It's the same with our carjacking weapon disarm techniques....these come so late in the game that we'll rarely get to them.

First, when in a car, stay the heck out of bad places. A friend of mine had a family member jumped while driving. He was messed up pretty bad. That's terrible but it was 3 a.m., he was in an area of town known for drug dealing and he was jamming his tunes with the windows down. I'd guess with even a little common sense he wouldn't have been harmed. If in a strange town never, ever get off at a ramp to park and look at a map or call for directions. Thanks to GPS people don't do this like we used to but many have been victims by parking somewhere they shouldn't have been.

Second, use the car. What would you do in this scenario? You are stopped by a biker gang and they are approaching you from all sides. Do you lock the doors and hope they don't mean real harm? Do you get out to talk? Go back to the previous blog on mind setting. You should have already thought about this scenario because you aren't going to come up with a plan now. My plan? I am sitting in a 3,000 pound blunt object. I am flooring the gas and going through them. I didn't start this and I assume I am about to lose my life....and all of my family members that are with me. Justified in my head!

Third, if someone jumps into my car with a weapon I jump out. No technique, no wrestling for the weapon. I jump out. If they are going to shoot me jumping out they were planning on shooting me anyhow. I might as well only give them one shot at a moving target! If I have my family with me? I use those cool carjacking disarm techniques, get his weapon and beat his rear end!!

I have talked about never being moved to a second crime scene in past blogs. You are always in a lot more trouble if you allow yourself to be moved. He is taking you to a place of seclusion for a reason. You are way better off, if he is in the car forcing you to drive someplace and making it difficult for you to jump out, to crash your car. Aim for a tree, parked car, building, etc. The harm you and your family take in that crash is nothing compared to the harm he has in store for you. You have also just given him the choice of staying around to harm you or fleeing because there is now help on the way. Police and fire department resources get to auto accidents in just a few minutes. Other bystanders are rushing over to help. Another thing to like about this is that you and your family were belted in, the scumbags usually don't take the time to do this!

Here is another scenario that needs to be pre planned for. Just because you are in a car and you see flashing police lights behind you doesn't mean it's a police officer. This has been done many times, especially to women. If you can't see the police car (usually they have a spot light in your mirrors) don't assume it's the police. If the cop doesn't look right or if you have any bad feeling at all it is always better to be safe than sorry. Yes, pull over but crack your window and simply tell the officer that you are afraid and need to know that he is a cop. A real officer should never be upset with a female who says this. The fake ones will scream and yell. Ask for a number to call to verify him or for the officer to lead you to a more public place. If he refuses I'd rather take my chances with a pissed off police officer than a scumbag who wants to do me harm. I'm fleeing the scene. If it is a real cop I guarantee you that several cars will be chasing you within seconds! Will you be in trouble? Yep. Does that beat what the bad guy has planned for you? Yep!

Again, pre plan and mind set. People are car jacked, forced into cars and forced off the road every day. This stuff happens, we must have a plan. While planning think about simply jumping out and/or ramming something with your car! It is better to be in an accident than to be moved…always!

Not In Traffic, Handgun From Drivers Side

1) Grab the weapon with whichever hand is closest/has a good angle and pin the gun against the dash.

2) Step on the gas and drive off. The idiot will let go or be dragged down the street.

Can't Drive Off, Handgun From Drivers Side

Most carjackers come straight on to the driver's window and stick a handgun in the driver's face.

1) Use the cupping defense. Redirect the handgun with the left hand and wrap the hand around the barrel. At the same time wrap the right hand around the hammer.

2) Sharply pull the handgun in and slam the attacker's hand on the dash, steering wheel, etc.

3) Torque the barrel with both hands back towards the attacker to take away. Make sure the barrel doesn't cross your body.

4) The attacker may run or you may be able to drive now. If you must get out to further protect yourself from the attacker:

5) Spin in your seat, put both feet against the door.

6) As you pull the latch stomp with both feet to swing the door into the attacker.

7) Unlatch your seatbelt and pass it over your head as you egress the vehicle.

8) Clinch and throw combatives.

This is easier to do in some cars than others. If you can't spin use your shoulder and arms to hit the attacker with the door. Law enforcement officers actually practice this...so should we!

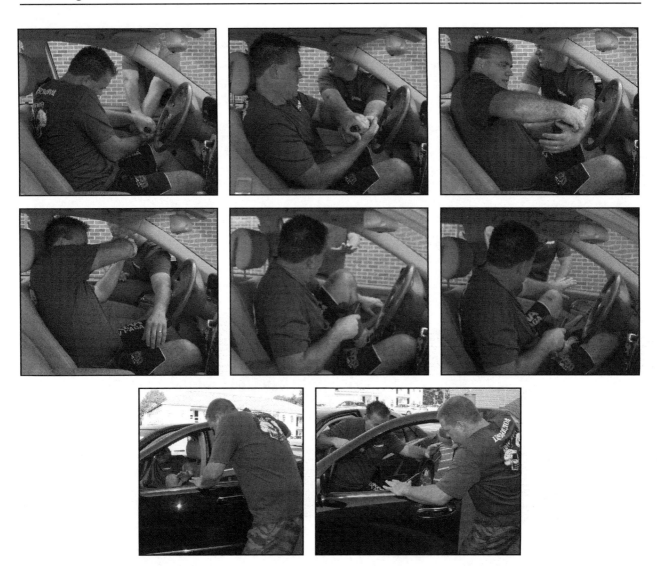

Can't Drive Away – Handgun From Behind Driver's Door.

When law enforcement approach a driver they don't walk straight up to the window. They come from an angle behind the driver. It is hard for the driver to turn enough to get to the officer in their seat and there is a door post in the way as well. Not that I worry about disarming an LE officer but the scumbags watch TV and study these tactics.

If the angle is good enough you can still cup and do the above disarm. If the angle is too severe you may have to:

1) Spin around and pin the handgun to the door frame with your right hand.

2) Worm the left hand up the best you can to cup the handgun.

3) Pull if forward, barrel pointing up so that it doesn't cross your head.

4) Continue with the cupping defense above.

Alternately, you may pin the gun to the doorframe with your right hand and beat the hand against the door frame. Wrap the wrist with your left arm and hug tight as you continue to beat the handgun against the door frame. Different cars may mean different tactics.

Blade

If the carjacker has a knife from outside the driver side window the above techniques are still applicable. Wrap both your hands around their wrist instead of the blade.

Can't Drive Off, Long Gun From Driver's Side

1) Grab barrel with both hands and rip the gun towards the passenger seat.

2) Attempt to get the long gun in far enough to push down and have the stock rest against the door so that the attacker can't pull back.

3) The attacker, if still holding the weapon, will now have his face in the window. Head butt, elbow, etc. until they let go and egress.

Alternately, if you cannot get the weapon in far enough to get stock on the door pull in as far as you can and, before the attacker can pull back, push down on the barrel so the attacker isn't pulling the weapon straight out but now has their wrists at an angle as you are putting weight on the gun. This isn't as strong as above but keeps them from easily pulling back. Strike the attacker until they let go.

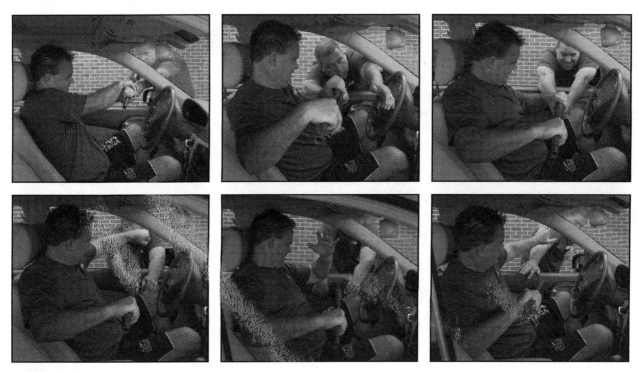

Attacker Jumps Into Passenger Seat

Don't ever leave your doors unlocked! Good idea but Murphy's Law applies to life.

1) Cupping defense, redirect and grab the weapon with your right hand, wrap the left hand around the hammer.

2) Pull the attacker towards you and head butt, strike with the barrel of the weapon, twist their arms ways they don't want to bend, etc.

3) Rip the gun out of their grip by twisting the barrel towards them, avoid crossing your body

4) Exit the vehicle.

If the attacker has a knife it is this same defense. Wrap both hands around the attacker's wrist and not the blade.

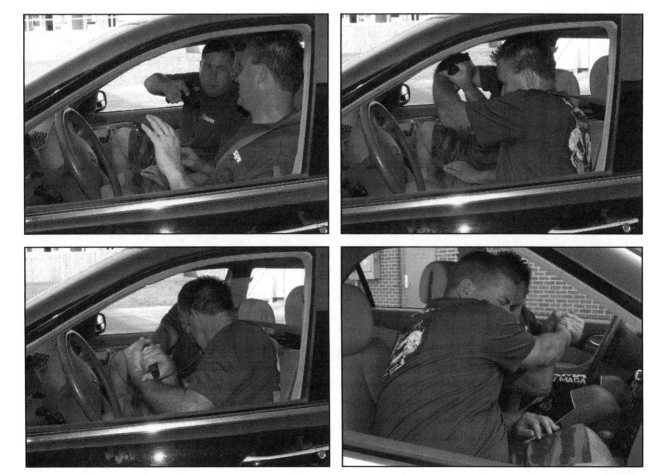

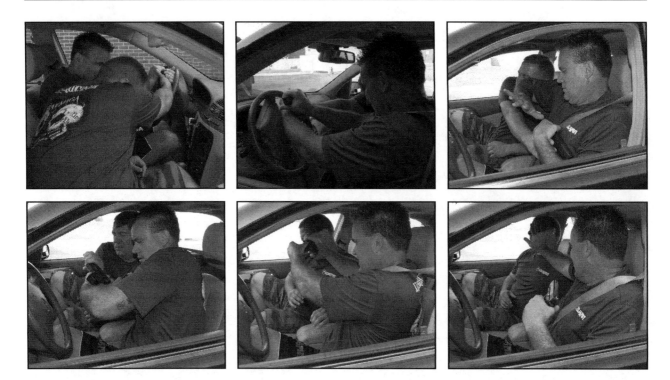

Attacker Jumps In Back Seat

Again, open the door and flee. If you cannot flee this is a tough one:

1) You must have the weapon close enough to grab. Fortunately, the scumbags usually try to intimidate with their weapon and will put it in your face/against your head. If pointed/touching the side of your head hook with your right hand and push towards the windshield.

2) Snap the handgun back towards you turning the barrel the opposite direction/towards the passenger door.

3) Get your left hand on the weapon and push again towards the windshield, slamming the weapon on any surface you can reach.

4) If the attacker still has the handgun quickly, when it feels like you won't lose control, throw the right elbow to the attacker's face and then get that hand back on the weapon.

5) When you have the weapon exit the vehicle.

There are a few scenarios that are downright frightening. You have your family with you and the scumbag gets into the back seat and puts a gun against your kids head demanding that you drive off or opens the passenger door and puts the gun against your wife's head and tells you to get out. Mindset these scenarios before they happen and have a plan. What can you do? There are no great answers. I am probably going to exit the car, but take the keys. He can't drive off now and may well get out to get the keys. I will under no circumstances allow him to drive off with my family members. If I have to I will dive over the passenger seat and attack the idiot. I may lose my life doing so but (pre plan these scenarios with your family) the wife will know that I expect her to drive off as I am scuffling with the scumbag. Of course, I recommend being armed, the scumbag is gonna get shot by myself and my wife!!

Long Gun

"After initial contact all plans go to hell"
—Patton

The first thing we do in long gun disarm training is tell both students (the partner doing the defenses and the partner playing the attacker) to grab the long gun. We tell them "when you hear 'go', fight for it". Invariably the students will play tug of war and attempt to twist the shotgun out of each other's hands. We then ask them if they have forgotten how to kick, knee, etc.? Let the assailant think tug of war, the student needs to be thinking "hurt the bad guy". As the assailant is tugging and twisting the student should be head butting, kicking and kneeing. The next think we do is similar. Lay the long gun in between two students and tell them "when I say go, get the gun". After they both dive for the weapon and one comes up with it we let them know that racing the assailant for the long gun is a 50/50 chance. While the assailant is thinking "go for the gun" we should again be thinking "hurt the bad guy". As the assailant is diving for the long gun, knee them in the face, you know where their face is about to be! Use combatives to put them down and then you have plenty of time to walk over and pick up the rifle/shotgun.

Long gun front

1) As your hands are up turn body and swat with right forearm over and slightly up to redirect the barrel off.

2) As this redirects the weapon burst off of your right foot delivering a punch or elbow to the face of the assailant with your right hand/elbow. Wrap the weapon with your left arm as

 153

you are striking, hugging the weapon tight so that it is pointed up. If you have a holstered weapon this is the time for a contact shot.

3) Raise your right elbow to shoulder height to get the weapon 90° from the ground and throw your shoulder forward to strike the assailant's face with the barrel.

4) As your shoulder is coming back slide your hand up the weapon to grab the barrel. Then either "kayak with anger" going forward and striking with the barrel and butt or strike to his outside shoulder as you pivot back and away on your left foot and take the butt by your right hip for the takeaway.

We used to teach a live side and a dead side defense. Our thought on this was that we could have someone on one side or the other of us, could be up against a wall, the attacker could have an accomplice on one side of us, etc. We would run a drill where the person defending would shut their eyes and when the gunman gave the command to open them they would decide which way they wanted to redirect (a partner would be on one side or the other) and then do the defense. Guess what we were creating? Hesitation. Hesitation will get us killed. We now honestly believe that the one time we end up with a rifle pointed at our face we will not be able to think of anything except "I'm about to die". We will not be able to think of reasons to redirect one way or the other. Under that stress and surprise a redirection will just come out of us, probably our right hand blocks if we are right handed and probably whichever one we practiced the most. The only reason we would teach someone to redirect with the left hand is if they are a left handed police officer or concealed carrier and their gun is on their left hip.

Left Handed Officer/Handgun Carrier, Long Gun From Front

Same as above, redirecting with opposite hand.

Gun From The Front Aimed Low

If the gunman has the rifle on his or her hip and pointed at your navel area there is a slightly different redirection. If your hands are up swat down with your left arm and continue to rotate that arm up you we burst in, ending with hugging the barrel to our body.

If your hands are down swat the weapon with the forearm of your right arm as you twist your body. This will send the barrel upwards. As it does burst in and wrap the barrel with your left arm.

Slung Long Gun Takedown

If the gunman has the weapon in a 1 pt., 2 pt. or 3 pt. sling it will be tight to their shoulder. This sling is designed so that if someone grabs the barrel the gunman can let go and access their handgun. After the initial burst and strike as you hug the barrel it will not point up but stay pointed forward. Strike several time and then burst off you your left foot to get behind the gunman to end up with your right hip bone on their left buttox. Take your right arm over the gunman's right shoulder and grab the weapon, the sling, a handful of clothing or skin or whatever you can grab. Pull sharply back on your right hand as you snap your hips forward, pulling the gunman down. Go down with and on top of the gunman so the barrel doesn't cross your body. Strike with combatives, draw your weapon for a contact shot, etc. Do not get up until the gunman is finished as you cannot take the weapon with you. Before you get up you can certainly unsnap the sling if you are familiar with the working or cut the sling off with a knife.

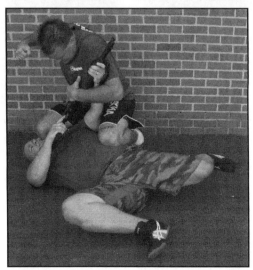

Long Gun, From Behind

1) Look over your left shoulder and continue the turn while swatting behind your rear end (as if a dog were sniffing there).

2) As this redirects the weapon pivot on and burst off of your right foot delivering a punch or elbow to the face of the assailant with your right hand/elbow. Wrap the weapon with your left arm as you are striking, hugging the weapon tight so that it is pointed up. If you have a holstered weapon this is the time for a contact shot.

3) Raise your right elbow to shoulder height to get the weapon 90° from the ground and throw your shoulder forward to strike the assailant's face with the barrel.

4) As your shoulder is coming back slide your hand up the weapon to grab the barrel. Then either "kayak with anger" going forward and striking with the barrel and butt or strike to his outside shoulder as you pivot back and away on your left foot and take the butt by your right hip for the takeaway.

Bayonet stab

This doesn't necessarily mean there is a bayonet affixed to the long gun, the attacker can simply be poking you with the barrel. Nothing changes from the long gun disarm other than you will lean forward as you hollow out your midsection and redirect as far out in front of you as possible.

Seminar: Long Gun Disarms (2-hour)

Both partners have both hands on weapon

Teach that bad guy thinks only "get the gun"–you think combatives and hurt the bad guy!

Gun at feet

Bad guy thinks "get weapon" – we think "hurt the bad guy". Knee as they dive/other combatives

1) From front

   - With own weapon, contact shot

   - Weapon aimed low, hands up and down

   - Show take away

   - Realistic attacker, sometimes on shoulder, some on hip

2) Jostle drill – One student is "it", one has the long gun the rest jostle the person who is it with kick shields. When the gun holder yells "gun" the pad holders get out of the way. The person who is "it" does the disarm. Go four quick reps per person.

3) Teach slung weapon takedown

4) Teach long gun from behind

Drill

Eyes closed – gunman from behind, front high, front low, front with sling – when gunman yells "gun" the student opens eyes and does the appropriate defense.

Multiple Attackers

*"No matter how enmeshed a commander becomes in his plans, it is
occasionally necessary to consider the enemy"*
—W. Churchill

Multiple weapon wielding attackers is certainly a nightmare scenario. The best bet is to run
like crazy! Punch a hole through them and keep going. There are times when this can't happen
such as you have a family member with you. This is why I, a Krav Maga "expert", am never
without a weapon myself. I carry a handgun where I legally can and always have a blade or
two on my person. There are no good answers to going up against several attackers with weapons when you have none. If this happens we have some tactics that may get you out alive.

- If two or three attackers are converging on you at equal distance the worst place to be is
where you are. That is where the attackers are converging to! You will do the last thing
they expect...attack them. IF there are three you do now want to go for the one in the
middle. That will put your back to one of the attackers on the side. Go for one on one side
or another.

- If they all have the same weapon (all have knives for example) you may want to go for the
smallest and weakest, the thought is that you can get their weapon. You may want to go for
the biggest and meanest. If you take him out the others may flee.

- If there is a gun you must go for that first generally. If you go for another you have to stack
and use that person as a shield.

- If there are one with a stick and one with a knife, go for the stick. Something with reach and impact is better than a cutting tool.

- As you are taking the weapon don't fall in love with the thought that you need that weapon. If another attacker gets close you may have to shove off and attack that attacker, push the person you are defending into the other attacker, lung over the attacker to strike the second, etc.

- You must stack. Spin the person you are defending against so that they are between you and the other attacker. Use them as a shield to strike over or to shove in to the second attacker. You must be able to see all attackers. An attacker you can't see is an attacker that knocks you out from behind.

- If attackers are at different distances, converging at different speeds you must attack the closest.

- You are always fighting to escape! You are not fighting to beat the attackers.

A few blogs on the subject from uskma.com:

Two on One

The last thing we do at the end of a level 3 test is to have the group gear up and spar...one student vs. two or three attackers at the same time. This is always an eye opener.

No matter how good we are two or more on one is a very bad situation. The first thing I do is yell "go" and then immediately yell "stop". I bawl the student out and tell them that I didn't give them any rules. The first thing they should have done was ran for an exit. The second choice, if there is no exit, is to run for a weapon. This isn't hero time, we aren't in a Hollywood movie, it is time to run for our lives! As far as a weapon goes there are things lying around everywhere that we can use. I tell them that I would rather smack someone with my laptop that's usually near me before I would go at them empty handed. Again, think escape first, get a weapon second. I've done martial arts and Krav Maga all my life and am fairly good but I can't see on both sides of my body, can't block four fists with two arms. Fighting isn't ever very smart, fighting when outnumbered is just stupid.

When it can't be helped and you have no other choice but to fight there are a few tactics to live by. At the training the ones who did the best kept moving, didn't let anyone get where they couldn't be seen and attacked when they could. Thoughts with these tactics are 1) for sure keep moving. The scumbags know that they need to split you, for one of them to get behind you. When someone is behind us we are finished. We cannot block or dodge what we cannot see. A punch on the back of the head is all it takes to be done. Keep your back to walls, etc as you circle…and you are circling to find an escape route. 2) Attack. You can't just circle and be defensive. Eventually they will hit you hard. Whenever one is out in front and closer to you than the rest hit hard and fast. Stomp a knee, punch the throat, kick the groin or anything else you can do to put them down. When this happens we have made the odds a little more even. Stacking is always a good way to have one closer to you than the other. Move so that one has to go through the other to hit you. Use the closest attacker as a shield. I have even seen grabbing hold of the closest with a choke, etc. and punching over them to hit the second attacker. Shove the one you have grabbed at the other, giving you space and maybe even knocking them over.

If weapons are involved you had better think of running first. Get out of there as the odds don't get stacked up against you too much more than this. If there is no escape we want to attack, not wait. They are converging on you where you are and expect you to stay there or back up. Do what they don't expect, go berserk and go after them. Go hard at the closest and attempt to take him out and take his/her weapon to use against the other. If one has a stick type weapon and the other a blade and are at equal distance, go for the stick. Reach and impact against that blade is a good thing. As you are taking the weapon from the first you must spin that attacker in between you and the other. Be vicious, like a cornered animal! As you are attacking always be looking at escaping. Do damage and get out of there.

In summary look to escape, find a weapon, keep moving so they don't split you and take the closest one out. The odds are still very much against us in this situation but these are the best answers we have.

A cool video on the subject:

http://www.youtube.com/watch?v=mWEroXIdGEg

Mob Violence

*"If violent crime is to be curbed, it is only the intended victim who can
do it. The felon does not fear the police, and he fears neither judge nor
jury. Therefore, what he must be taught to fear is his victim."*
—Lt. Col. Jeff Cooper

After showing a video on our Facebook page of a mob attack in Memphis this week we had several comments on what to do. I put a video on the page on what I would do...here it is written down:

These gangs of usually teenage boys, when they decide to randomly attack strangers, are involved in what SGT Rory Miller in his books Meditations on Violence and Facing Violence calls the "group monkey dance". This is a dangerous dynamic. They are looking at who they attack as below them, not part of them and have no more remorse for their victims than you or I would in killing a snake. They are showing loyalty to the group by taking part in the violence. Even more terrifying is the fact that the more violent and crazy they act the better their reputation in the group is. This is why you see people who are already unconscious continuing to be kicked in the head, etc.

The concepts I try to get across on this subject are run away, you can't win when outnumbered, carry a weapon and when it's go time it's time to get mean and nasty all come to play now.

First, of course, is don't be there. The quote my friend John Burton uses all the time is "Don't go to stupid places with stupid people to do stupid things". You know where the bad parts of town are, don't ever go there. Keep your head on a swivel because the bad parts of town may come to find you when you are someplace not so bad. We are all decent people, we pride ourselves on not being prejudice, being color blind (cue the music to "I'd like to teach the world to sing") believing that we are all created equally, etc. but guess what, the scum bag thugs are some of the most prejudiced people on the planet. This is why they are scum. There are scumbag whites, blacks, Hispanic...this isn't a race thing, it's a being a piece of crap thing. If you notice that you are suddenly in the minority where you are at and being looked and pointed at, keep your eyes peeled...as you leave.

Don't be like most of America and bury your head in your phone to answer that oh so important text. Keep your eyes open and observe everywhere you go. Always be vigilant watching for groups forming. Watch for people talking while their eyes dart to you. Watch for pointing or anything that just doesn't look right. Don't ask yourself what doesn't look right and try to figure it out, leave. As soon as you feel the least bit uncomfortable, leave.

If you see the attacks start and you aren't targeted yet, run. Yes, there is a time to intervene and help those being attacked but when outnumbered fifty to one adding another body to their count isn't helping.

When they start to approach you it's go time. We don't wait to see what they intend to do. As soon as even a few start towards you put your plan into action. Your first plan, again, is to run. Run now and run fast. If others are with you, they should know the plan ahead of time. If you are cut off or have family with you it's time for part two of the plan. You escape by going through. You get vicious and mean and do the most damage to anyone close that you can. You clear a path and get out of there. Being on the ground is death, if you get knocked down do as much damage as you can to those around and get up! There is no talking your way out, no reasoning. These are scum bags who don't look at you as human, they look at you as entertainment. In our seminars on this subject we show a video of some news footage of a family that was attacked by a mob. As they beat the husband the wife was pleading with one of the attackers to stop. He turned around and punched her in the face. We are dealing with animals and we must become an animal.

In this vein, nobody can fight twenty people and win. This ain't Hollywood. Cops can't be everywhere. Cops are only minutes away when seconds count. If you are going to survive this it is up to you. Do what I do…carry a handgun where it's legal and a knife all the time. I'm not talking about a small apple cutting knife, I'm talking about a pig sticker. We've already decided it's go time. The only way out of this mess is to be more violent, nastier and dirtier than the scumbags. This isn't the time to think about not hurting anyone, what the police will think, etc. You will eventually be let out of prison, you're in a casket for good. Here's my plan. If it's the knife I attack. I don't waive it and try to intimidate a path open. The scumbags all have knives I'd bet…and handguns. Go for whoever is closest and stab them in the face. Go right down the line stabbing any face you see as you clear a path. If they are not running away they are a threat to your life. They may eventually take me down but I guarantee I won't be the only one bleeding at the end. If it's the handgun with me that day…same plan. I shoot the closest person in the face and I get out alive.

Brutal is what Krav does best. Mind set and have a plan…think about this stuff before it happens. Tell yourself that "I will go home today no matter what". BE SAFE!

Getting Krav Maga – Blogs From UKSMA.com

"When a wolf bites a sheep the sheep bleats, rolls over and dies. When a wolf bites a sheepdog the sheepdog gets pissed off and bites back."
—Col. Grossman

Lessons From The Bus

At a recent USKMA affiliate training we did "Krav on a bus".

Lessons learned from defending on a bus:

There ain't no sparring. Sparring is footwork, changing distances, moving, etc. On the bus there was no room for footwork whatsoever. It was close in, clinch and flail away. When kicks were there at all they had to be linear. No looping roundhouses, spins, etc., just straight kicks and then not with power because there wasn't any room. Basically it looked like a hockey fight.

Ground…what ground? Our BJJ guys found out there was ground techniques only if we fell perfectly down the aisle and hit the ground…and then we were wedged and not exactly able to change positions. If you were mounted, you stayed mounted! Some of the attempted arm bars, triangles, etc. worked every now and then…until there was a second attacker. BJJ, like sparring in general, goes out the window on the bus.

Krav Maga's choke defenses, bear hug defenses, hair grab defenses, full nelson defenses, etc., etc. didn't translate well to those close quarters. There was NO room to move, to throw the attacker away from us, to get side clinch to throw knees, etc. the way we can if we are in a gym.

Hence, the reason for all the preaching that techniques can't be relied upon. The philosophy of "get rid of the danger and destroy the attacker" paid off. Those being attacked figured it out. They got the attacker's hands off their throat and turned the tables with fingers in the eye, biting, elbows in the groin and the like. They made me proud!

The same goes for knife and handgun. Many of those techniques didn't translate to "I am pinned to the window in my seat by the moron sitting beside me who froze as the guy behind me is stabbing me in the head". As with chokes, etc. the techniques weren't there but the philosophy was. If it was a knife it was "don't get stabbed, hit the idiot". Block that blade as best you can and punch the idiot in the throat, ram a finger in his eye, elbow his head so hard he looks like a PEZ dispenser. In most videos we watch of those being attacked by a knife the poor person getting stabbed fixates on the knife trying to grab the attacker's wrist and never attempts to hit the attacker. Again, we were proud of what we saw! With the handgun it was point the barrel somewhere besides at me (or others) and hit the idiot. Technique didn't happen but that philosophy kept people alive!

Scenarios. These were cool. In a bus full of people I would point to only one or two and tell them they were Krav students and everyone else on the bus was just going to sit there and scream. We would have one or two attackers board the bus and attack with a knife or handgun. Sometimes the attacks were random and directed at everyone and anyone, sometimes they had a specific victim. We saw some cool things. The Kraver figured out how to get to the attacker through the rabble and neutralize the attacker. Some things learned were:

- Going for the knife hand was hard, that hand is swinging up to 5 feet as the attacker slashes or stabs. The arm pit stays in the same place. Start there and slide to lock up the rest of the arm.

- Wrapping the knife or handgun arm and waiting on the crowd to jump in and beat the attacker works….unless the frozen goof balls don't help. Then it's a fight!

- The attacker that jumped on the bus with a hand grenade threw us all for a loop. Nobody said it was going to be only a knife or handgun! Even the kravers kinda froze for a bit there. Wrapping the hands before the spoon was released wasn't easy. Hoping to beat him down to the ground with the thing under him when it went off was sometimes the only thing to attempt. Don't ride the bus was what we mostly learned there!

- We aren't the savior of the world. When the scenario was two obvious gang bangers got on the bus and started knifing a passenger that was an obvious gang banger as well we still had the kravers going to rescue the one being attacked. I talked a lot about knowing what your go buttons are beforehand. If I see that scenario I am going out the back door. I will then point to the lady with the kid and tell them, come on, I'll help you off, then the next lady, then the next person, etc. from outside of the bus. Why would I put my life in serious jeopardy to stop what was obviously gang related. I wasn't going to save the dude's life, he would have taken 30 stabs by the time I got to him. My go buttons tell me that if it's a woman or a child being hurt in any way I will intervene. If it's obviously an innocent being ambushed by more than one, I've told myself I'll do something in that event as well. If a law enforcement officer isn't obviously winning a fight I will jump in and help. However, if it's two dudes beating on each other or something that looks gang related, I'm not putting myself into that.

Smarter Than IMI?

If you have read our book American Krav Maga you know that we don't claim to be teaching Imi's Krav Maga (Imi Lichtenfeld is regarded as the founder of Krav Maga). The United States Krav Maga Association is teaching a self defense system based off of Krav Maga's philosophy and techniques. Every now and then a fellow Krav Magaist will take offense to this. I get asked things like "Oh, are you smarter than Imi?" Well, Imi was a legend and a genius. He came up with a system that is very effective, easy to learn and uses our body's natural reactions. I certainly will never say that what I am doing is better than what Imi came up with. I do know that nobody, other than Grandmaster Yaron Lichtenstein , is teaching Imi's Krav Maga. Most systems are teaching Israeli military techniques and calling it Krav Maga…and then arguing over who is doing it the way Imi wanted. Imi truly wanted Krav Maga to be Israel's martial art. After retiring from the military he started developing Krav Maga for civilians…and only then was it called Krav Maga (around 1974 was when the name was introduced). He wanted students in gi's, bowing, calling the techniques by their Hebrew names, etc…just like every other martial art. Imi's Krav had some flashy moves, high kicks and other things that you would associate with a traditional martial art.

There is no military or police unit in the World still training the same techniques that they trained in the 1950's and 60's. When a tactical group cross trains they see other ways of doing things, they then put their heads together and make it even more effective. Years of seeing what others are doing and testing things in the field means that military and police tactics and techniques keep evolving. A martial art can keep teaching the same techniques the way they were shown hundreds of years ago. That is the art and they are "respecting" the founder. Trouble is, what they are teaching isn't cutting edge self defense, it is an art. To think that the way a defense was done a thousand years ago is as good as it can be and it should never be changed is silly thinking. We in the USKMA scour the internet, attend seminars, read and watch everything we can get our hands on to keep making our system more effective for those who practice it. I do not look at this as disrespecting Krav Maga's founder, I look at it as taking very seriously the job of keeping people as safe as possible.

Also, in America in 2014 we have to think of techniques and tactics for things that didn't exist in Israel in the 50's and 60's. There probably weren't many carjackings, for example, at that time and place. We must have answers for those now. For some reason I learned quite a few knife defenses when I was learning Krav Maga but never saw one for being shanked or a hockey punch type of attack. Those are the ways criminals today attack people. Baseball bats, recidivist home invaders, curb stompings, etc. are common in present day America and virtually unheard of in 50's Israel I would think.

Techniques that I was taught when I learned Krav Maga that we have changed recently include:

- Machine gun takedown. We have kept these in the system only for a few handgun scenarios. These were developed right after WWII. We have all seen the WWII movies of the German prison guards with the machine gun slung over their shoulder and hanging by their hip. This was designed to spray a room. The defense for this made sense at the time. Nobody carries a slung weapon on their hip today. Today the sling is tight around the shoulder to fire the weapon from the shoulder and designed so that if someone grabs that weapon to let go and access a handgun. We have a defense for this type of sling now that wasn't needed fifty years ago.

- Long gun defenses. I was taught one for live side, one for dead side and one for from behind. These were all as different as night and day from each other and had a lot of moving parts. We now teach basically one defense that works for all of these attacks.

- Knife defenses. I was taught a lot of knife defenses that included grabbing wrists. I never felt that any of them were a good answer. In the gym with a half-hearted attack they worked ok but as soon as someone attacked aggressively with a sewing machine needle type of attack they went to pot. When we add KY jelly, baby oil, etc. to our arms and try these techniques they hardly work at all. These slippery substances mimic blood. If there is a knife there is probably blood flowing. We want to train for worst case scenario so to ignore the blood while developing a technique could be a deadly mistake. We take both of our arms and wrap and hug the attacking arm with all of our knife defenses now. Training and watching videos of actual knife attacks has shown us this is a better answer.

- Knife held to neck. I was taught that if the knife is on my right shoulder side to push it towards my right shoulder and then disarm with a cavalier and the exact opposite if it's pointed towards the left. This works in the gym but on the street with the stress of "I'm about to die" how can I know which way it's pointed? I can't see it. If it's pointed towards my right and I push it left I slice my own throat. I'd say in the real world with stress and adrenaline I have a 50-50 chance of slicing my own throat...those aren't odds I liked! We now collapse down on the knife holding arm with both of our arms (hugging the attacker's arm to our body) to start our defense. This works whichever way the knife is pointed.

- High kicks, spinning kicks and jump kicks. We moved them way back in our system...to black belt. Imi wanted them in the system so we kept them but we see no reason to have them early in our training. The time spent to get good at these techniques is better spent on basics. Basics is what will save us in a real encounter!

- Baseball bat swing stick defense. We have pretty much stopped teaching this. When we taught the two defenses (overhead and baseball bat) and had the attacker choose which they would attack with the practitioner always hesitated a split second to decide which defense to do. We are safer if we just go in...do the overhead defense no matter what they are swinging. Hesitation gets us hit and if we guessed ball bat and its overhead we get our head's split open.

- Hair grab from the front. Why complicate this? If they grab your hair from the front kick them in the groin or punch them in the face. They'll let go.

- Handgun disarms. We have taken out the "pin the handgun to the hip and punch" that most systems do. The cupping technique is our answer to handgun from the front. It is a better and stronger technique. If I am teaching a two hour handgun disarm seminar to a small female officer it could take the whole two hours to get her a decent punch...and then I wouldn't bet on her hurting a large man with it. The cupping has a front kick to the groin. I have no faith that she can pin that handgun to a large, muscular and enraged man's hip. The cupping has her keeping both hands on the weapon and using leverage. It is also much easier to go "off hand" with...it's ambidextrous. The beauty of this technique is that we learn it for gun from the front and then there is nothing to change (so that we can learn very quickly) for handgun front on knees, mounted, from side of head, from guard and standing over.

Our only purpose in what we teach is to keep people safe. We teach (in this order) to stay away from bad places, to run, to pick up something to use as a weapon and, as a last resort, to use Krav Maga. We teach the most battle tested, real world techniques that we can find...and then tell people that techniques won't save them. Our main goal in class isn't to teach techniques but to give people a switch to go from overwhelmed, confused and uncomprehending to going forward with hatred and rage to do the maximum amount of damage in the minimum amount of time. As I've blogged many times, ask any cop whom they would rather face. Their first choice is a very proficient black belt martial artist. Their second choice is some crazy who wants to claw off their face and chew their eyes. They would pick that martial artist every time. If we can make our practitioners the crazy (when they needed to be) and give them skills we are making some very safe people indeed. We are getting people ready to defend the type of random violent attacks seen in the U.S. Getting people ready for the gang tactics, weapons, home invasions, car jackings, rape attempts, beatings, etc. that we see in the U.S. BE SAFE!

Why?

Why do we do things the way we do in USKMA classes? I get asked this from time to time. When I do instructor training for new affiliates I give them a specific template for running classes. All USKMA gyms across the nation are pretty much teaching classes the same way. I emphasize that there are two reasons for everything we do in our gyms. Reason 1 is that whatever we do must make people safe. Our job is to save people's lives. We will teach the most battle tested, cutting edge, effective, easiest to learn and easiest to recall self defense techniques and tactics that we possibly can. Reason 2 is to get people in the door. We teach a fast paced class, emphasize the workout and weight loss aspect and truly compete against the big box gyms, not martial arts schools. Showing gym owners how to grow a business is important, profit isn't a dirty word. Now, we will not compromise one of these for the other. We will not teach "fluff", water things down, take it easy or make an aerobics class out of our classes. That may get more people in but we will not teach anything that is BS just to make money. Likewise, we could run classes like an IDF boot camp. I know gyms that do this. We can go overly hard, make beginners practice outside defenses without padding to "toughen them up", injure people, scream and belittle the whole time, etc. If we did this we would have tough as nails, studly students...all ten of them. I cannot make people safe who are not in class. Why would I have ego to run classes like this to make ten people safe when, if I do it right, I can make hundreds and even thousands of people safe? When I owned gyms in Columbus, OH we had 750 members, 660 of them were adults. If you took one of our classes you left pretty sure that we weren't taking it easy, that it was real self defense and that you were just ran into the ground. We didn't do fluff but we also weren't sadists. Below are questions I've been asked with two part answers. One part is why it's done to make people safe, the other part is why it's done to get people in our gyms.

WHY ARE CLASSES SO BASIC/SO MUCH PUNCHING AND KNEEING? 1) Basics will be what saves our butts if we are ever attacked! I know of three of my black belts who have been attacked over the past few years. One ended the attack with a punch, one ended the attack with an elbow and one hit the attacker with a six pack of beer upside the head. They all verbalized to me that they were disappointed, they all had this vast bag of techniques in their brains and that's all they did. I told them that that is the point. The basics, done well, is what it's all about. It is funny that most well known MMA or BJJ fighters who put out DVDs have "advanced techniques" on them but when you watch them fight they only do basics. This is why they are champions, they do the basics better than anyone else. If it's complicated, it isn't self defense!

2) As a workout in class a ten combination attack would be slow, have to be demonstrated many times, have to be slowly added to and slow class down. A ten combination that is six punches, clinch and throw four knees is more effective, won't have hesitation as we try to remember and anyone can do it after being shown once.

CAN WE SLOW THINGS DOWN AND WORK ON TECHNIQUE? 1) Nope, techniques won't save your ass, going forward with rage and swinging for the fences will. Techniques degrade under stress, a bunch. If I can guarantee that this technique is going to pretty much fall apart if you are attacked (and have that adrenaline dump, blood pooling to your core due to vasoconstriction, brain jumbled and not thinking or remembering, etc.) why would we want to emphasize the technique in class? What will save us is having a 'flinch' reaction that has us going forward with hatred and rage to do the maximum amount of damage in the minimum amount of time. This is why classes are all about aggression and heart and why everything we teach is put under exhaustion and stress. 2) That's what they do in martial arts class. How many adults are lining up to get into those?

WHY DO YOU HAVE FITNESS CLASSES AT YOUR GYM? If you study self defense and read books that interview survivors of vicious attacks (Strong On Defense by SGT Strong, Meditations on Violence and Facing Violence by SGT Rory Miller) you will see two truths. One is that the first person to go balls to the wall generally wins. Two is that the person who exhausts first usually loses. If you can fight harder for a longer period of time than the attacker you are virtually unbeatable.

2) If we have a martial arts dojo and add Krav Maga we look like a martial arts dojo with a Krav class. If we have Krav Maga, CardioMMA, Crossfit, etc. in our gym we look like a fitness and self defense Mecca! Give members three of four things to attend every single day. The box gyms don't tell members "you can come twice a week for this one hour class". Since we are competing against them, neither should we!

WHY DO YOU HAVE OTHER CLASSES SUCH AS MUAY THAI AND BOXING AT YOUR GYM? Our gyms had a BJJ class, a Muay Thai class, a boxing class and an MMA class every week that our members could attend. Beginners certainly needed Krav Maga if they were there for self defense but they could hit these other classes as well. Their hands could only get better if they went to the boxing class, their ground got better with BJJ, kicks got better with Muay Thai, etc. Our advanced students in Krav Maga were certainly encouraged to hit every-thing. If all things were equal who would be better able to defend themselves. A ten year Krav

Maga student or a ten year Krav Maga student who also had several years in BJJ, boxing and Muay Thai? Yep, that's how we saw it as well.

2) When it was time to sign the agreement to join the gym we got a lot of "You mean I can do all of this for this one price?" That's called adding value to their membership.

WHY DOES EVERY CLASS HAVE TO END WITH THOSE DAMNED DRILLS? If we, God forbid, are ever attacked on the street we will be stressed, confused and exhausted. If we learned techniques but never had them put under stress, confusion and exhaustion we didn't prepare for what a real attack is. We don't know how our body is going to react. We are freezing because we don't understand what is going on. We learned self defense techniques, not self defense. There is a big difference! These drills are the best thing we do for self defense in class. No time to think about technique, just hit the target! We can hardly breathe, stand or lift our arms but we are still fighting...we are going on heart! If ever attacked on the street we will have a "been there, done that" feeling!

As people are crawling out the door completely spent they will shake your hand and tell you what a great class that was! That is a workout! We have had many, many members over the years lose 60, 70...even 100 pounds. We made them both safe and healthy!

MEAN AS SIN. "Hey man, what art do ya study, what system you in, what techniques do ya know, who'd you learn from....wow, you're a tough dude!" No, being a tough dude makes you a tough dude. Going forward, going hard and being mean as sin is what wins a violent confrontation, not what you know. It always makes me laugh when someone asks me who would win a fight between an (insert martial art here) vs. an (insert other martial art here) expert. I also get a chuckle when told that someone who studies (again, insert whatever here) would take a Krav Maga practitioner in a fight. I always tell them that the Krav Maga practitioner could well lose. It's not about the art studied as much as it is about the individual fighter and his/her mindset. Yep, that's right...the art isn't as important as the mindset. Generally if the guy who wins a fight had been a practitioner of BJJ, Muay Thai, Krav or anything else he would have still won. This is exactly what we are talking about when we tell people that there are no magic techniques. Krav has the best, most battle tested techniques anywhere but they won't make anyone unbeatable. What wins a fight is an aggressive "I will not lose, I will keep fighting no matter what" mind set.

When I am told that someone doing (insert) hasn't lost a fight, is a bad ass, etc. I always reply that they would be a tough person and a good fighter no matter what they were using as a defense system. It's way more about the fighter than the system. A tough guy with a "won't lose" attitude is going to usually win no matter what he is doing. A high level Krav Maga instructor recently made the statement that the toughest guy he knows, the guy who has been in and won more fights than anyone he has ever met has no training whatsoever. He went on to say that he is studying this guy more than he is studying any techniques from any system right now…it will make him better.

It's all about attitude, aggression and craziness. I have said many times that if you ask a cop whom they would rather face A) a very proficient martial artist or B) some nutso who wants to rip off their face and chew on their eyes they would all pick the martial artist A good example of this is a story the co-lead instructor of the USKMA, SGT Brannon Hicks, tells about his toughest fight ever. The one who was kicking his ass (and he's in more fights in any given month than most of us are in in our lives) was a fifteen year old, 90 pound female meth head. He says she was as mean as sin! She clawed his face, tried to bite his groin, spit on him, kicked and punched non-stop and was doing more damage to him than about any other person he ever fought. Good thing he had backup!

The point is, what you know, what you studied, how much you practice, etc., etc. is nice but in the real world what saves you is swinging for the fences and being "mean as sin". When I am asked what my definition is for self defense I say "Being able to go from overwhelmed, uncomprehending and terrified to instantly going forward with hatred and rage to do the maximum damage in the minimum time possible…and then getting out of there."

Why Krav? We learn great techniques but also let our students know that techniques aren't magic. We spend a lot of time developing the "can't lose" mindset. Making people aggressive when they need to be, developing the "flinch" reaction of "go forward and go hard", finding the switch to flip to go from overwhelmed, afraid and frozen to attack mode is what people need to be safe. Techniques are secondary! BE SAFE!

What I Did In Martial Arts Class

What I did in martial arts class…and why it was pretty worthless for self defense

This isn't a put down to those doing martial arts. I spent a big chunk of my life doing martial arts. I currently have my son in martial arts. I believe it is great for kids. For adults it is great exercise, good for self discipline, balance, coordination, a fun hobby and a cool thing to spend time getting good at. What I have a problem with is when a martial art claims to be the ultimate in self defense.

I feel that I am pretty qualified to talk about both the martial arts and self defense. I started a "traditional" martial art in 1986. I won a national title in sparring, coached many national medalists and champions, spent many years teaching martial arts and was a fourth degree black belt in the art. In the late 90's I started hearing about Krav Maga. I saw Krav Maga at a martial arts show and was fortunate enough to be in one of the very first Krav Maga instructor training programs in the U.S. I am now a third degree black belt in Krav Maga and travel the country teaching the system to gym owners and law enforcement groups.

The stuff we did in martial arts class:

BOARD BREAKING PRACTICE. We would take a kick and practice it for three or four months and then break a 1x10 piece of pine with that kick at our belt test. As we travelled up the ranks we would put on a show with our board breaks, breaking several boards with several different techniques. Why we spent so much time on that I'll never know. At tests and tournaments we would spend five or ten minutes just setting it up. We had to have several holders, tell them just where to stand and how to hold and would run through it in slow motion three or four times before we ever started. The holders had to know what they were doing and not move at all. What were we preparing for...a fight against a bunch of mannequins? Those great, powerful kicks and strikes were never practiced dynamically. Never practiced against something that didn't want hit and was hitting back. We certainly weren't fighting smart and stacking attackers, the boards were on all sides of us.

KATAS: There are martial artists who can make a pretty good case for practicing katas...I hated them even when I was in the art. I was told they had several uses, one was practicing techniques. I am not sure how practicing to the air and not full speed was getting me ready for anything. I'd rather have been hitting heavy bags and mitts with power. I was told it was practice for multiple attackers. If that was true why in the hades did I keep turning my back to the guy I just hit? Why was I not stacking and moving dynamically and running away? To practice certain blocks and then punch and kick combinations was hoping that an attacker would come at me and strike in the pattern I was training. Hope ain't a strategy!

ONE STEP SPARRING: Maybe the most worthless thing we ever practiced. I would get into a front stance, perform a low block with my front arm and chamber my back arm at my waist to punch from there. My "attacker" would then do the same. When I kiapped (yelled) he would take a step and punch from his waist to my chest and freeze there like a statue while I did my defense and counter attack. WTF!! This is screwed up on so many levels that I don't know where to start! If I am ever attacked on the street it would be nice if the attacker gave me space, didn't attack until I let them know it was ok to do so, kept their hands down, punched at an area that isn't fragile, froze after one strike and stood there to let me do something back. If I had that attacker it wouldn't much matter what I practiced for self defense! As Rory Miller says in Facing Violence "100 defenses to 100 attacks works for sparring, not ambush...and then it takes years of practice."

TECHNIQUES: We were focused only on techniques. The martial arts are about the only thing you'll find that works and works on answers without ever knowing the question. To work on defenses for attacks you would think that you would study violence and see how the scumbags actually attack. We had 30 defenses for a straight knife attack to the midsection. Say what? Hick's Law tells me if I have more than one choice it takes time to decide between them. How much time do I have when a knife is coming at my gut?

When we practiced our kicks we would do 100 reps with each leg and then move on to something else. We never practiced with an attacker, with stress or exhaustion, while trying to hit something that didn't want hit and was hitting back or with an attacker's buddy approaching fast. We practiced self defense techniques but never once practiced self defense. Under stress I am sure I would have thrown one kick, stopped and re set and then threw another…just the way I trained.

We practiced for hours in front stances for me to learn later that they were developed for balance when fighting on ships. We spent hours in a horse stance for me to learn later that this was how peasants, who didn't own horses, practiced for the cavalry. Our high flying sidekicks were developed for knocking people off horse back. A lot of time spent learning how to defend myself against things that I would never run into in modern day America.

FREE SPARRING: Our sparring was kicks only and high and spinning kicks counted for more points. We feinted, circled, came in and went back out and danced for most of a two minute round. Sparring on the street is stupid. For one, sparring distance is run away distance…or pick something up to smack the idiot with distance at least. Self defense is going forward with hatred and rage to do the maximum amount of damage in the minimum amount of time and then getting to safety. If you are sparring the idiot's buddy is closing in on you. Every asshole has an asshole buddy close by!

If you want to practice martial arts, do so. Just don't confuse them with self defense. If you are wanting only to learn to defend yourself look for a self defense program. If it's fancy, it isn't self defense. BE SAFE!

Just Run Away

When there was trouble Forrest Gump ran! This was a brilliant tactic as it kept him safe (even kept him from being fried in 'Nam). When I give lectures on self defense the first thing I tell people is "don't be there…don't go to stupid places with stupid people to do stupid things". The second major bit of advice I give is "run". Run away, run to help, run to pick something up to use as a weapon but just RUN! When I teach knife defense seminars the first thing we do is practice sprinting away from someone who is going to their pocket. The second thing we practice is punching the dude going for his pocket…and then running. These are the best two knife defenses I have. Running is generally the best thing to do for your safety! If the local paper has me on the front page with the headline KRAV MAGA EXPERT RUNS FROM KNIFE I wouldn't be offended. I would see that headline and think "a still living, very smart Krav Maga expert runs from knife"!

But let's think about this advice. Can you run? When is the last time you did any sprint work? The average violent criminal is a male ages 18-25. Can you outrun a young dude who is still in his athletic prime? I doubt I can anymore. Are we fit enough to not keel over dead after attempting to run thirty yards? Do we just hope that we are attacked only by overweight, slow and lazy people? Hope isn't a strategy. So, first point of running for safety is to get yourself into shape. This is why we are so physical in our Krav classes. This is why we recommend to our affiliate gyms that they add CardioMMA and Crossfit. Techniques won't save anyone. Being in better shape than the attacker, going off with rage, going forward and going hard is what will save us.

Next thought: What are you wearing? Most guys I know, when they go out, are in athletic shoes. Most women, however are in things I couldn't even stand in, yet alone walk or run in! During self defense for women seminars I talk a lot about this. Those "cute shoes" could be your downfall. How can you outrun anyone in those stiletto heels? Statistically violence tends to happen more often where young men gather and where minds are altered. This sounds like most bars, doesn't it? If you are going to the bar those cute shoes may not be the thing to wear. How quick can you get them off and run barefoot? The second point is to plan and mind set. Wear things you can fight and run in…have a plan!

Last thought: Where are you running to? Again, have a plan and mind set. When you go into a restaurant, theater, etc. you should not only know where the exits are but also should have put yourself in position to get to them quickly. If outside in a city do you know where you can run to most likely get help? How about out in rural areas. Where can you run to quickly where help is available? In our self defense for women seminars I make the point that a tazer isn't to be totally relied on. When you taze the guy it will lock him up for thirty seconds…if both barbs got him (happens less than 70% of the time). How far can you run in thirty seconds? When it lets go of him he may well sprint to wherever you are to do you harm.

So the next time you hear someone say "I'd just run (like Forrest)" ask them what shape they are in, what they are usually wearing and, in their plan, where are they running to. Thinking about these things ahead of time gives us a plan. Plans don't get made up under stress but the plans we have do surface and our training will come out of us. BE SAFE!

Can I Do It?

When I owned gyms I got calls from all sorts of people who wanted to know if they could learn Krav Maga. They thought that they might be too old, that their physical problems might keep them from being able to participate or they may have even had a handicap. My answer was always "Krav Maga would be perfect for you".

The history of Krav Maga shows how it was developed for everyone, not just athletic people. Imi Lichetenfeld was put in charge of the IDF's hand to hand training when Israel became a nation in 1948.

Problems that Imi had that are great for us today are that he had, in the IDF, both men and women, ages 18-55 and he had everybody, no matter what shape they were in. Because of that you'll see no jump, spin, flying anything in Krav Maga, you'll see a lot of groin kicks! Also, he had recruits for only six weeks. Because of all of this Imi had to teach things that didn't rely on brute strength or size because he had small women to train. It had to be easy to learn and easy to remember because he had them for such a short period of time. If you know anything about Israel, it had to be effective. Krav Maga isn't a Martial Art where things are done because of tradition. Israel doesn't care about tradition, they care about survival. If something comes along easier to learn or more effective they'll jump to that technique in a heart beat.

I told these people who thought that they may not be able to participate in class that their age, physical problem or handicap didn't automatically keep them from being a victim of a crime. In fact, it may have actually increased the odds. They would be able to do most of what we teach because whatever we teach in Krav Maga has to be effective for the smallest, weakest and most un-athletic in our classes. To have defenses that use size or strength to be effective is ignoring those who need self defense the most.

I would tell them to sit out of anything that looked like it would aggravate their problem or anything that looked too rough. If they only did half of each class they would still be learning self defense and become safer than if they didn't do anything.

When I trained people who were missing an arm, for example, it really paid off that Krav Maga is much more a system about a philosophy and not techniques. Having only one arm would keep a student from perfecting a technique that takes two arms. They would never learn it correctly. However, the philosophy of "go off, go forward, go hard and destroy the attacker" is something we can all learn to do. Hitting with what ya got, blocking with what ya got and being full of rage will keep you safer than any able bodied black belt in a technique based system. In fact, for our level five test I make the students do the first half (it's about a 4 ½ hour test) with one arm tied to their body. They have to figure out what to do with choke defenses, knife defenses, handgun defenses, etc. My thought is that their arm may have been shattered first thing in the attack. If they had only learned techniques they would be at a major loss only being able to use one arm. As it plays out, they all do great. They make it up on the fly and keep aggressive. I get to see a lot of head butts and knees!

Everyone can't become a black belt in Krav Maga but everyone, no matter what their handicap, can become safer. Don't let any excuse get in your way! BE SAFE!

Self Defense Class?

There are several things that I see in most self defense classes that I don't agree with. Am I right and everyone else wrong? Nah, I don't have the ego BUT here are some things to think about.

Warm ups. I don't like wasting time! When I teach a class I feel that I have 50 minutes to make all in attendance as safe as possible. I have been to classes that warm up for half an hour. I always felt that I was there to learn Krav Maga, not do pushups. I can do those at home. We warm up for 7 minutes in classes I teach. In those warm ups we do "Krav" motions so that I can correct and work on form. Punching and throwing elbows will warm up shoulders. These are motions we want reps on because they make us safe. Arm circles, etc. warm up shoulders as well, but we aren't repping anything we'll actually use in self defense!

Learning techniques. My opinion is that there are no magic techniques. Techniques will not save us in real world violent attacks!! I tell students "Aggression is our number one technique. Aggression and going totally off like a crazy person is the number one thing to work on to keep us safe in the real world." I have read several studies that seem to indicate that between 75 and 90% of martial art black belts who get into a real world fight...lose! When I read this as a martial artist I was offended. Now that I can look back I see how this can be, I see the flaws in the way I was training. The martial art that I was involved in was a lot of "technique training". We would practice a kick on a target for many reps. We never worked on hitting a target that was moving and didn't want hit. We never practiced on a target that was trying to hurt us. We never had a plan for what we would do if that kick didn't devastate the target. We didn't practice a philosophy of "go hard until the target is down", we just practiced a technique.

Class pace. This goes along with the above paragraph but to not run people into the ground in class is a mistake. Everything we teach we put under stress and exhaustion. If we are ever attacked on the street I can guarantee that there will be lots of stress and exhaustion. To rely on anything that hasn't been practiced under the circumstances we'll face in the real world is a mistake.

Drills. This is the most important thing we do in class for self defense. We go as hard as we can with multiple attackers for 1 to 2 minute rounds. This is gut check time. We may not be hitting as hard at the end of the drill as we were at the beginning but we are still hitting! We will outlast the scum bag. NO matter how tired, cramped, etc. that we are we will not quit until the threat is down. We will keep going no matter what! BTW, when running drills make it hitting things, not calisthenics. As my friend and 2nd degree Krav black belt Matt Kissel says "I've never had to do a burpee in the middle of a fight". Train for what you'll see.

Knife on Knife, stick on stick, etc. training. If someone has a knife I don't want to fight them with a knife. Heck, if you are in a fair fight your tactics suck!! I want a ball bat against a knife. I'll take a ball bat and an attitude over a black belt in any system! Even better, I'll take a handgun and distance. We actually train handgun quite a bit in Krav Maga. I'll argue that ten hours of handgun training makes us safer than 1,000 hours training with any other weapon. We need to teach people to run from weapons. Most of the weapon vs. weapon training that I see has a fatal flaw…they are one against one training. Every asshole has an asshole buddy close by!

Training tools. The training tool that is popular with Krav people that I don't get are the shock knives. They don't hold up that well, are expensive and…pretty friggin worthless in my opinion. What is the reason to use shock knives (or the old put lipstick on a rubber knife and wear a white t shirt)? Are you saying that if you get touched by the knife you didn't do the defense right? I call bullshit on that. In a knife attack you are going to get cut. We don't even call it "knife defenses" in our seminars, we call it "knife survival". If you are doing defenses and not getting touched by the knife I can guarantee you that the attacks aren't realistic. We expect to get cut, we are trying to avoid the 40 stab wounds to the chest that the average psycho is attempting to deliver. I've also been told that the "shock" mimics pain and teaches us to keep going when we feel it. I would suggest that people who believe that go study the adrenaline dump and stress. You ain't feeling pain under the stress of someone trying to kill you…that comes later!

A much better training tool for knife defenses would be KY jelly. Any defense you are teaching should be able to be used with that stuff slathered all over your arms and hands. There is blood on the scene of almost every knife attack. Blood is one slippery substance. If the defense can't be used effectively all slicked up like that it isn't a good defense. Guess what, most every defense you know for a knife fails under that test. What works best? Punching or kicking the attacker as hard as you can as you attempt to block the blade…and creating distance to get the heck out of there or access a better weapon (such as a ball bat).

Instructors, when people come to you for self defense training they are literally putting their lives in your hands. Train them smart, train them for what they'll see. BE SAFE!

Shmuck Kwon Do Is Better

I am often told (by well meaning folks who are proud of their art) that a certain technique they are doing is better than what we teach in Krav Maga for a particular situation. I am even told that entire systems or arts are better. My response is "It may well be but what exactly do you call 'better'". In Krav Maga the only thing we claim to do better than any other system is to take people from zero to being able to defend themselves quicker than anything else. So to us, quicker is better.

Take Krav Maga's knife defenses for example. I am often told that there are way better knife defenses out there. I say that there may well be better, but at a trade off we can't do. Say that I have a grouping of Knife defenses that are indeed a bit more effective than what we teach in Krav Maga but they take 100 hours of practice to be proficient with. My other choice is some pretty simple yet fairly effective defenses that can be pretty much mastered in four hours. In Krav we take the quicker to learn. Most adults don't have years to dedicate to perfecting an "art". They need the basics to protect themselves with now. What if in hour 99 of practicing knife defenses someone puts a handgun in my face? The way Krav is set up in that 100 hours of practice time I've gotten down knife, stick, handgun, unarmed attack and many other defenses.

The next thing to worry about with the other guys "better" defense is for whom it's better for. It may work fine for that big ol' ex-Navy SEAL instructor but how does that translate to the five foot, hundred and two pound female in his class. Whatever we teach in Krav Maga has to be effective for the smallest, weakest and most un-athletic in our classes. To have defenses that use size or strength to be effective is ignoring those who need self defense the most.

Back to knife defenses. I hear often that doing the Krav Maga outside defense against a very trained knife fighter is a mistake because he will pull back and cut the arm that we blocked with. I ask them, well, what would work with an experienced knife fighter? I would guess nothing much. To dedicate years to being good with a knife isn't going to pay off if you come up against a guy who is better. I have heard that the top ten Filipino knife masters of all time all died the same way…from knife wounds. Ya know what we have in our system? A handgun course. I'd argue that you are better off with ten hours of good range time than 100 hours of training with any other weapon!

Now, when I am told that there are better handgun disarms than what we teach I get a bit lippy. I tell them that if what they do is better, more reliable, quicker, easier and more effective than what we teach it would already be Krav Maga. We would have stolen it from them!!

When people say what they are doing is better it usually boils down to one thing. It is what they do…so it has to be the best. I always laugh because if, when they were six, their mama's would have put them in a different dojo then that art would be the best! When asked "doesn't that apply to what you do" I say "nope, we don't have a system that is unchanging and must be blindly followed. We have the luxury of ditching a technique and adding something new if it is easier and more effective". We in Krav Maga actually use critical thinking, look around for better and put everything under stress and exhaustion to see how it would hold up in the real world.

Tueller Drill

We do this very drill with law enforcement officers in our LE training. We have one officer with a training knife five feet away draw that knife and sprint towards the other officer to see if he can get his handgun out of the holster and trained on the attacker before being stabbed. We then repeat at ten feet, then fifteen. When we finally move the attacker back far enough that the officer can get his sidearm out and trained on the attacker we remind them that one shot isn't going to knock the attacker off his feet. We have videos we show where an attacker takes ten or more shots mid body and keeps stabbing and slashing. Most officers know that they need to be twenty-one feet away to draw and fire on an attacker with a knife before that attacker can get to them. This number has actually been moved to thirty feet, twenty-one feet was where the officer was winning half the time. They finally realized they needed a number where the officer was winning most of the time!

Now the problem is, if this is shown to officers (or anyone else) we must make sure that the right lessons are being taught. The knife guys usually smile and say "See, knives are where it's at". Well, the lesson is that the guy with the knife can stab you if they are within thirty feet before you can put them down. The lesson isn't that the knife guy wins. If you stab someone but still take several shots midchest, that is not a win. At best it's a tie. What is your goal there, to have "I got him too" on your tombstone?

For the officer the lesson isn't "I will shoot him but if he's within thirty feet I'll get stabbed". Unfortunately I've seen this taught and that was pretty much what the officer was left with. What exactly are they supposed to learn from that? The lesson I would want to get into the student's head is that "yes, if a guy with a knife is within thirty feet and he charges at you and you do nothing but stand still and put both hands on your handgun to fire it, you will get stabbed…so don't do that!"

How about some tactics! Learn that when you draw on a person that has a knife to start moving, circling, creating distance, etc.! The time to practice this isn't when It happens but in training. To always fire on a line at a target and never move isn't training for what you will see in the real world, it is training to shoot a target that doesn't move. The other horrible training flaw I see is that officers (or civilians) practice putting thousands of rounds down range with their good two hand grip. Under the stress of an attack that same officer will not be able to think but will fire exactly how he trained. I have seen videos where an officer keeps firing away at an attacker that has a knife as he takes stab after stab. If that officer would have just let go of the weapon with his off hand and blocked that knife, the outcome would have been much better. Again, we need to train firing one handed while blocking a knife, stick or punch with the other. Train for what we'll see, not to hit bulls-eyes on paper more often than anyone else.

As I've said many times, if someone is within three feet of me I'd rather them have a handgun than a knife. However, I'd still rather have a handgun than a knife for myself no matter what the distance! Don't show cool videos and do cool training drills without figuring out answers. A drill to teach "wow, this is scary" won't do us any good when it gets scary! There is no unwinnable scenario when it comes to training to save you and your family's lives! If you are in a fair fight your tactics suck!

Americanized Krav Maga?

As you know by now we don't claim to be teaching Imi's Krav Maga (Imi Lichtenfeld is regarded as the founder of Krav Maga). The United States Krav Maga Association is teaching a self defense system based off of Krav Maga's philosophy and techniques. After training with Grandmaster Lichtenstein in Israel (and bringing him to our gyms in the states) I realized that nobody, other than he, was teaching Imi's Krav Maga. Most systems are teaching Israeli military techniques and calling it Krav Maga…and then arguing over who is doing it the way Imi wanted. Imi truly wanted Krav Maga to be Israel's martial art. After retiring from teaching in the military he started developing Krav Maga for civilians…and only then was it called Krav Maga (around 1974 was when the name was introduced). He wanted students in gi's, bowing, calling the techniques by their Hebrew names, etc…just like every other martial art.

When I trained in Israel with the Grandmaster it was almost like a bizarro parallel universe. We taught to keep hands up to block, they taught to keep them down to invite the attacker in. We taught to twist our core and use our whole body to develop power in punches, they taught to use arms only but to toughen up your knuckles by punching brick walls every day. We kicked to the groin with any part of our leg or foot we could hit it with, they got angry at this claiming that kick was to only use the ball of the foot. We taught to kick to only the liver and below, they liked high kicks…even high spinning kicks. We keep things as simple as possible, they had some rather flashy and fancy techniques. It went as far as we wore cups, they didn't and would kick you on purpose in the groin if they knew you were wearing one.

Was our way wrong? Was theirs? No, it was all about who we are teaching. They are used to tough as nails, macho Israelis in their classes. They can be all about bravado and keep their hands down, can punch walls, can basically be training to be the baddest dude in town and win a stand up fight with anyone. That is their way, the way they think. In the U.S. I certainly can't teach my small females using that way of thinking…or anyone else really. If I trained people that way I would have very tough students…all ten of them. When I owned gyms in Ohio we topped out at 760 members with 670 of them being adults. We were teaching a lot of people to be safe! To train the average U.S. citizen to be safe isn't about brutal training to make them tough. It's teaching them to win no matter what. We teach them to cheat, to kick to the groin, to hit from behind and to hit non-stop until they are safe. If we are in a fair fight our tactics suck! I have often said that if a master from BJJ or Muay Thai came to my gym and challenged me to a fight me in front of my students they would probably kick my butt. If that same person were in my house and going to hurt my family, I would not lose. I would hit them from behind with a chair, take one of the broken shards from that chair and shove it down their throat. I would do whatever it took to keep my family safe.

Our only purpose in what we teach is to keep people safe. We teach (in this order) to stay away from bad places, to run, to pick up something to use as a weapon and, as a last resort, to use Krav Maga. We teach the most battle tested, real world techniques that we can find…and then tell people that techniques won't save them. Our main goal in class isn't to teach techniques but to give people a switch to go from overwhelmed, confused and uncomprehending to going forward with hatred and rage to do the maximum amount of damage in the minimum amount of time.

As I've blogged many times, ask any cop whom they would rather face. Their first choice is a very proficient black belt martial artist. Their second choice is some crazy who wants to claw off their face and chew their eyes. They would pick that martial artist every time. If we can make our practitioners that crazy (when they needed to be) and give them skills we are making some very safe people indeed. We are getting people ready to defend the type of random violent attacks seen in the U.S. Getting people ready for the gang tactics, weapons, home invasions, car jackings, rape attempts, beatings, etc. that we see in the U.S.

Mental Toughness

I haven't seen Survivor in years but there was a time I wouldn't miss an episode. One of my favorite challenges each season was when they would see who could be uncomfortable the longest. They would do something like have the group stand on a log and see who would last the longest. This was really nothing hard, just stand there and keep your balance. Well, it was always funny to see that the least mentally tough would be done in an hour while the winner would go on for ten, twelve and even more hours. The most athletic, strongest or even the youngest wouldn't win. The mentally toughest would. It was most often a woman, which always intrigued me.

In Laurence Gonzales' great book DEEP SURVIVAL (highly recommended along with Ben Sherwood's THE SURVIVORS CLUB) he tells the story of Debbie Kiley. Debbie was on a yacht, the Trashman, that sank at sea. Before the accident happened she told of how the Captain and his first mate were heavy drinkers and actually drunk when they sailed. She goes on to talk of the first mate's girlfriend and how helpless she acted. It seems the only people doing all of the work were Debbie and another crew member. After the accident they all got on a small raft that was being severely tossed in the storm. The two who kept control of their thoughts and attempted to think of solutions (Debbie and the hard working crew member) were rescued many days later. The other three died during the ordeal. The difference? Mental toughness.

If you really want to read about mental toughness get some of the books written by the Viet Nam war POW's. One story I read recently was that of Jim Thompson. After being captured Jim was forced to live in a small wooden cage that he could neither sit up in nor stretch out in. Several months later he was moved to solitary confinement…for four years! Finally he was moved in with other prisoners, but of course the torture and beatings continued the entire NINE years! Oh, and during all of this he managed to escape five times, only to be recaptured and tortured some more. Fellow prisoners at the time thought he was a corpse in the next cell as he weighed all of ninety pounds when he finally was released. Other POW's facing the same treatment didn't last six months. Jim's mental toughness was immeasurable! Sadly Jim did die…30 years later, of natural causes, in Florida!!

I love watching the Ultimate Fighter. You can pick the mentally tough ones out early…and the not so tough. They all think that they want to be in the UFC, think they are bad dudes. It seems like the ones who do all the talking about how great they are, how they'll die in the ring before losing and how losing isn't an option are the first ones to just stand and freeze in the ring or purposely give up their backs so they can tap out. The mentally toughest usually last the longest in that show and, I would think, in a true violent situation.

I don't care what techniques, system or art you are learning, if you aren't building mental toughness you won't last long when confronted with real world violence. I would bet on a mentally tough person with little training in a horribly violent confrontation way before I would a black belt from any system or art that isn't mentally tough. This is why you have heard me say many, many times that it isn't the art, system or techniques that will keep us safe if violence ever finds us. It is attitude and mental toughness. This is why Krav Maga is based on philosophy and not techniques I don't care what techniques you know if you don't have the "flinch reaction" of go forward, go hard, go now and go until the scumbag is down. Even if injured, even if outnumbered, and even if afraid for our lives we go off with rage and swing for the fences.

This is why when students in class ask me to slow the class down so that they can learn the techniques better I tell them "no". Those techniques won't save them. Learning to keep going with the stress, exhaustion and not knowing what's coming next in our drills is what will save them. Developing mental toughness is way more important in keeping our students safe than any of those cool techniques!

Knife Fighting!

A conversation with one of my black belts about how the USKMA's black belt and 2nd degree black belt curriculum is so sparse is what got me on this subject. He asked if we would ever include more offensive knife. I know of other Krav Maga curricula that have a ton of stuff in the upper belt curriculums…a ton of unrealistic stuff thrown in there just to have techniques to keep teaching. I always felt that if Krav Maga is supposed to be easy to learn and easy to remember as well as designed for real life violence there wasn't a whole lot of need for multi-attackers with chain saw defense, urban warfare tactics or complete stick and knife fighting curriculums.

In the USKMA 2nd degree black belt curriculum we do have some offensive knife/knife vs. knife. It is exactly four moves. If I am being attacked and must protect myself and my family and have a knife with me I only need to know where to cut to stop the attacker and how to deliver that cut. Why make it complicated? As Bruce Lee once said "I do not fear the man who has practiced 1,000 kicks one time, rather, I fear the man who has practiced one kick 1,000 times." If we had a whole system for knife there would be a lot of "fluff". Krav Maga doesn't do fluff! My cop friends tell me when they see surveillance videos of knife attacks, even from trained knife fighters, it ends up being the same slashes and stabs that anyone else would use. Stress and adrenaline bring out the basics.

Don't get me wrong, the knife fighting arts are deadly. If there was an offensive knife instructor in my town I would go take lessons. It would be cool and a ton of fun. However, of the three or four self defense scenarios that I can think of off the top of my head knife fighting doesn't make a lot of sense for any of them.

Scenario one would be a knife against another weapon. I have said many times that if an attacker is close to me I would much rather him have a handgun than a knife. However, at ten feet and out I would much rather they have a knife. If I were to carry one or the other it would be a handgun. I've heard knife guys say that they would slice me up before I got to that handgun. Well, that's a silly thing to say. There are too many variables that they couldn't know beforehand. Did I start first, see it coming first, have distance on my side? Am I the aggressor, have we started after already injured, etc., etc.? Yes, I know of the Tueller drill. I may well get sliced as I draw that gun, may even receive a fatal wound. I would do this as I am putting ten hollow points center mass. What would have been your goal…to have "I got him too" on your tombstone?

Scenario two would be an unarmed attack like a bar type altercation. If someone is punching you and you slice them up I would imagine that you are going to jail and being sued. You would certainly have to prove to the jury that you were afraid for your life to justify the use of a deadly weapon. As soon as they find out you train Krav Maga that's out the window!

Using a knife against multi attackers would be easier to justify in court. I'd still rather have a handgun than a knife in that situation.

Lastly, using a knife against someone who has a knife really isn't anything I'd want to do either. I would rather have a ball bat or something similar that would give me reach and impact. Better yet, I'd run. Even if I had practiced offensive knife a bunch it would still be a gamble, the other guy may be pretty good too. The old saying "The one who wins a knife fight is the one who dies the next day" I would think is too true. I have been told that the top ten Filipino knife masters of all time have all died the same way…knife wounds. If they all died in a knife fight what makes me think I'll get good enough to be unbeatable? Knife fighting would be too even of a fight. We always want to have the advantage in Krav Maga. If we find ourselves in a fair fight our tactics suck!!

So no, we won't have a whole knife fighting curriculum in USKMA Krav Maga anytime soon. Practice the few moves we have and keep it simple. That's our way!

Paranoid

"And so as you hear these words telling you now of my state. I tell you to enjoy life. I wish I could but it's too late."
—Ozzy in "Paranoid"

"It is not paranoid to think that there are people out there who may try to kill you if there are indeed people out there who may try to kill you."
—SGT Samford Strong

I am told quite often by friends and family that I am paranoid. I don't argue much because I am! For many years I was a paramedic/firefighter and saw the results of accidents and violent crimes first hand. When I started teaching Krav Maga I decided that if I was going to help people become safe I needed to study exactly what I was making them safe from. I studied real world violence, criminals, horrific crimes, home invasions, psychology, etc. to the point that...I am pretty friggin paranoid!

There are sociopaths out there who don't look at you as human, they look at you as entertainment. There are scumbags out there who can torture and slaughter your whole family and then go laugh about it. As Stanton Samenow says in his book Inside the Criminal Mind "No matter how a sociopath was made, once made there is no rehabilitation."

From a blog I wrote a couple of years ago about criminals: "Scumbags are good at what they do. Most have a system down that they follow time and time again, because it works for them. If you are attacked there is an 80% chance that it will be by a recidivist. A recidivist is someone who has been in prison for a violent crime in the past that has been let out (hooray for our awesome judicial system). He has a long list of victims. He will not change for you. You are not human to him. You are a resource. He sees you as the means to an end...you are money, the car, the rape, etc. Begging, pleading, trying to reason, etc. will not work because, again, you aren't human you are just next. The recidivist considers themselves more important than their victim and their wants more important than following societies rules.

The recidivists do not look at consequences. Jail doesn't scare them. They live for today because they really don't expect to live a very long life. Prison is a stop to get medical care, food and shelter. They will continue their victimizing in jail, it's just a change of scenery to them with a new victim pool. This criminal's sense of right and wrong is grossly distorted. There is no remorse, no regret and no hesitation to use violence as an end to a means.

Predators are patient to get what they want. They will wait and attack from the greatest advantage they can find. They weren't loved or nurtured, were abused, had a rough life. This makes the bleeding hearts want to "educate and rehabilitate them". These people can't be helped and don't want help. They hate life and hate you.

I'm the type who craves knowledge. I refuse to believe things just because that's what I was told to believe or because it's easier to believe. I'd rather be paranoid than have my head in the sand! Most victims of horrible, violent crime never thought that it would happen to them. My wife, back in our dating days, had a job that had her working odd hours and took her to many different cities. One night on the phone (about mid night) she told me that she was going jogging. I assumed she met on the treadmill at the hotel. The next day I asked her how her jog went. She told me that she ran by a seedy looking bar that didn't look safe so she turned back. My jaw hit the floor…and I griped at her a good bit! She is a 4.0 college graduate and pretty darned smart. To do something like that was stupid. She was the type that just thought bad things happened to other people. Now that she has a kid and has lived with me for several years she is a bit more "paranoid"!

Paranoid keeps me looking around. Paranoid keeps bad habits from forming. Paranoid keeps me vigilant. Paranoid is a good thing! BE SAFE!

Choose Your Weapon

"The iron hand ain't no match for the iron rod."
—Bob Dylan

I have said before that a person with a small amount of training and a weapon will defeat an unarmed person with an expert amount of training the vast majority of the time. We self defense "experts" and martial arts black belts don't like to hear such things but if you think about it this is just common sense.

I know many "good" unarmed knife defenses. I have trained them for years. I am a fourth degree black belt in Taekwondo and a third degree black belt in Krav Maga but if faced with a knife wielding attacker I'd rather have a ball bat than all of that unarmed knowledge.

Ask a cop who they would least like to come up against by themselves. Choice one is a very high ranking and very proficient black belt in any art or system you can name. Choice two is a psycho crazy with a machete. I would guess the majority of law enforcement draw their side arm and shoot the crazy!

Last one. You have to walk through a tough neighborhood at night to get to safety. You can bring your black belt buddy with you or you can bring your buddy who has a bowie knife. I'd guess you bring the one with the weapon.

I wrote an article once about martial artists and handguns. The point was that I believe the old martial arts masters from centuries ago would have spent time on the range getting good with handguns and cut way back on their training time with sais, kamas and nunchucks.

Every now and then I get someone who wants to learn Krav Maga at our gym who just doesn't have the physical ability. Either age or handicaps have made it hard for them to move. I will teach them Krav Maga, of course, but our emphasis will be on using a blade, or better yet, a handgun. Weapons are the great equalizer. The attacker can be much bigger, stronger, athletic and even have way more training but a weapon will give us the advantage.

Anyone testing for black belt in the USKMA must have taken an NRA gun safety course. The reason is twofold. 1) If we are learning to take handguns away from someone we certainly need to know what to do with it once we have it. 2) Being proficient at Krav Maga AND being proficient with weapons makes us one hard target.

Suck It Up Buttercup

Years ago, before we were married, my future wife came to my gym to watch me run a higher level Krav Maga test. I am basically a jerk when I run tests…just mean. As people were dehydrating and falling down with calf cramps they would hear "Get up and fight or get the f$%& off my mat!" and "You want to quit, go ahead. Maybe I'll run a test for sissies later this month!" among other things. When someone gets kicked in the groin and drops to the ground during a test or class I say "hey everyone, look! This is why we kick to the groin…it works! Now get up." On the way home after the test I noticed she wasn't talking to me. When I pressed her she blurted out "You're an ass!" I had to explain to her that I know those people were hurting. Calf cramps and groin shots are friggin painful. I want to push people past what they think they can handle. I told her "I am not holding people's hands to get them to the next level so they can feel good about their accomplishments, I am teaching people to survive things that would force most people to give up. I am making tough people!" She gets it now, she'd just never studied real world violence or knew how to train for it.

It drives me crazy in class to see people stop when they get a busted lip, a side cramp or the like. Now, I was a paramedic for many years, I know what a serious injury is. I will take people off the mat if they pull something, get knocked silly or are bleeding. However, it's poor training to stop with any little injury. In my opinion you are training to stop when someone makes contact with you when you do that. Guess what, in a real attack there will be all kinds of contact! I had a cop in my level 1 classes years ago that got popped in the nose. It wasn't broken, wasn't even bleeding but he dropped to the ground and got into a fetal position. I was livid! I yelled "Get the hell up! The scumbag is now taking your handgun and shooting you in the head!" He was offended and never came back but I didn't care. He was doing something in training that would have gotten him killed on the street. Pathetic!

Most martial arts classes if you hit someone you stop and apologize. What kind of training is that? That will come out of you under stress. We are training to hit people...hard! I have trained myself as I demo and make accidental contact to keep going. I'll say "oops, got ya didn't I" as I continue to beat on my partner. If it was a really hard shot I'll apologize to them...after class. I've also trained myself to take it and keep going. It happens to me often but the two that stick out in my mind are the time I was demoing a drill and the student who was demoing with me elbowed me in the face so hard that I blacked out on my feet for a second. I kept talking and explaining the drill but I must not have looked too good, several students came over and grabbed me and told me to sit down for a few minutes. Another was during my black belt test. During handgun defenses my partner punched me under the eye so hard it split the skin. I grabbed a paper towel that someone handed me and kept doing my handgun defenses one handed until the blood stopped pouring. Now, I am no tougher than anyone else, I just train correctly.

I used to train often with Olympic Gold Medal winning boxer, Jerry Page. When we would spar I would, every now and then, actually hit him. One time I said "Jerry, I actually hit you" and he just laughed. He said "I'm standing in front of you, you're gonna hit me every now and then. I never was in a bout that I didn't get hit several times in each round. I know how to roll with punches and, when I do get hit hard, I don't show it. I'm coming after you!" I likes that attitude! When I first was getting in to self defense (before MMA became popular) I heard a speaker say "the dudes I see who take a sucker punch in a bar and get back up are boxers. They train to do that. Most everyone else lays there like they're dead." Train to take shots and keep going!

Now, we can't be brutal in class and purposely hit people. We do, at the end of level 2, start to introduce sparring. Guess where the big fallout is...not many test up to level 3. We introduce sparring correctly, are as safe as possible and don't let people get hurt but still, not many students want to do it. I tell them we spar for two reasons. 1) Self defense isn't always someone comes up to choke you, it could well be someone squaring off with you and throwing bombs. 2) The best way to get used to getting hit and keep going is to get hit and keep going.

If we are ever attacked on the street we will probably get hurt. I tell my students to accept this right now. Say it and know it. Now, tell yourself that I will probably be hurt but I will pay it back times ten! Injury is coming, decide on who's terms it will come. Next time you get dinged in the gym keep going…suck it up, Buttercup.

WHAT WATCHING 'CHOPPED' TAUGHT ME ABOUT SELF DEFENSE

I don't watch much TV…mostly History Channel and the Food Network. My favorite show? Chopped! I am into cooking…but that's not important. What is important is what we can learn from this show (which is about people using "mystery" ingredients to cook something good in 20 to 30 minutes) about self defense. It seems like in every other episode one of the chef's cuts themselves with a knife. They are professionals who use knives every day. They almost always say something like "what an amateur move, I haven't cut myself in the kitchen in years"…and yet it happens on this show time after time. What is the difference for them cooking in this competition compared to cooking at their restaurants? Stress. They are nervous, trying to hurry, stressed and often their hands are shaking. So, these motions that they can do in their sleep become much, much harder under stress. They screw up, can't do fine motor skills and make mistakes.

This reminds me of the first deer I tried to shoot. I'm not a big deer hunter but my brother-in-law is trying to teach me. When we were sighting in the rifles I could hit a dot on a paper plate every time at 200 yards. Just put the crosshairs on the dot and pull the trigger, piece of cake. The day I had a buck in my sights was a bit different. He was walking away so all I saw was his butt and didn't really have a shot and that's probably a good thing…because the crosshairs were jumping all over the place. I couldn't figure out why I couldn't aim. Afterwards I realized that my hands and forearms were aching. I was evidently squeezing the rifle so hard that I couldn't hold it still. Stress had affected me to the point I couldn't do what I had trained to do… and that was just a deer!

It was just a deer that I was hoping to shoot. It was no threat to me, it wasn't attacking me, it wasn't scary and yet, a big adrenaline dump and stress. Imagine the stress of someone trying to slash you with a knife. Knowing that you may be dead in the next few minutes, fighting for your life, worried about what he does to your family if he gets through you. I have blogged a lot about real world violence and how stress effects our bodies. Blood pools to our core making our limbs heavy and numb, hearing and vision get messed up, odd thoughts enter our mind, we can get stuck in a loop where we keep doing the same technique over and over even when it's not working, time can distort, we'll could well lose bladder and bowel control, etc, etc.

You can probably guess where this is heading. Those who teach self defense have got to keep everything simple using gross motor skills and train everything they are showing others under stress and exhaustion. There are a lot of cool looking things taught in martial arts and self defense classes. Cool doesn't translate to being able to pull the same technique off when it's for real. Krav Maga teaches aggression, gross motor skills, whole body movements and to go forward with all you have and end the attacker any way possible. Any techniques that relies on joint manipulations, fine motor skills and precision will fall apart in a real attack. Those fancy, complicated defenses just don't work under stress.

I once saw a handgun defense taught that included sticking your finger behind the trigger, between the trigger and the trigger guard. Yes, technically that will keep the gun from being able to fire. This worked for the instructor as he demonstrated it with his assistant who stood there like a statue. If done in a real attack with the stress involved the chances of this defense being pulled off is right around zero. Trying to hit that small target while not being able to judge distance, hands shaking and arms feeling heavy is an impossible task. Yet, it was taught to others by a "professional". This kind of thing pisses me off to no end! This "professional" instructor is teaching things to people that will get them killed. Not realizing the effects of stress, exhaustion and adrenaline while showing people "gym techniques" is inexcusable. If it's your job to show people how to be safe you had better study this subject ad nauseam.

RBT

"If you aren't putting everything you train under stress and exhaustion you are training self defense techniques, not self defense. There is a big difference."
—M. Slane

We just finished the USKMA Pistol, Patrol Rifle and RBT (Reality Based Training) Development Course for law enforcement officers in Colorado. The shooting at the range was fun….the RBT training will save lives.

In RBT we padded up, used sim rounds and set up scenarios. Very fascinating to watch! Adding realism and the stressor of pain (those sim rounds sting) equaled stress, adrenaline dump, and exhaustion in those participating. The first time through everyone got stuck in the loop, saw things that didn't happen, had time compress or expand, got clumsy, did things that didn't match up to their training and, generally, performed poorly. It was an eye opener for all to see what that stress and adrenalin did to us. Listening to the description after the scenario by those involved was amazing. They thought they saw things that weren't there, described that they "fired when he reached for his weapon" but clearly didn't on video (the bad guy fired first), didn't have a clue how many rounds they fired, stated that it seemed to take over a minute for their round to go from the barrel to the bad guy, etc., etc. This was amazing training!

The cool thing is that the more we repeated scenarios the better the officers performed. One comment after a scenario that involved an innocent who jumps out of a doorway showed this training to be gold. The officer stated "I aimed at the innocent but didn't shoot because I had been there before and recognized it." The first day he shot an "innocent" who surprised him. By the third day his reaction saved the innocent because he had been through that before… two days earlier. The scary thing is that a lot of departments don't practice this way. The first time the rookie officer sees a scenario is when he is living it. How crazy is that?

Everyone involved absolutely made mistakes the first time through. If the first time through is for real it can cost lives.

SGT Brannon Hicks, who taught this course and is one of the top RBT instructors in the U. S. says that in SWAT school they did a week of nothing but scenarios like this for 15 hour days. The first time through they all sucked…and they were SWAT operators. By the end of the week they were a well-oiled machine…even with the total exhaustion.

Thoughts when designing RBT scenarios:

- Go from simple to complex. The first time through we wouldn't put an officer through several stressors and three assailants. We would start with 1 static role player (RP). Then we would go to two static role players. Then one static and one dynamic RP and finally two dynamic RP's.

- Clear scenarios that teach a specific lesson. The RP, for example, may be told that if the officer leaves cover you raise your weapon and fire. IF the officer stays behind cover you stay compliant.

- The officer wins. Do not run no win scenarios. The RP's job is to lose. IF the officer makes mistakes we reset the scenario and run through it until he wins.

- Mistakes will be made. We don't "teach" by saying "you should have done this!" We ask leading questions so that the officer comes to their own conclusion. This will keep them from being defensive and feeling that they are being picked on. Approach it with questions like "Who did it benefit when you left cover, you or the assailant?" They can't argue when they are the ones who make the statement.

We have got to train for what we'll see! We must put everything we are doing under stress and exhaustion. This is what we do in USKMA Krav Maga classes. The fast pace, the drills and the way we test is centered on creating stress, exhaustion and the adrenalin dump. When someone is attacked on the street by an aggressive, angry, screaming idiot we want our practitioners to have the "been there, done that" feeling. Practicing handgun defenses, for example, against a partner smiling and standing still like a statue isn't what we'll see on the street. When we pad everyone up and have the partner swearing, threatening, striking the practitioner, waving the handgun around and being aggressive we are creating what the practitioner will see on the street. Now, when it happens it isn't the first time they have seen such a thing. Again, the beauty of RBT is that when it happens to us we will have been through that aggressive attack many times in training, it will not be our first time through the scenario. Train right, train often and BE SAFE!

Ch- Ch-Ch-Changes!

We in the USKMA look hard into what other arts, systems, instructors and gurus are teaching as far as self defense goes. We attend seminars, host instructors from other systems at our gyms, buy books and videos and generally study everything that's out there. This makes our system better. We don't have the ego to think that we are doing everything the very best way possible 100% of the time. Being closed minded wouldn't make the USKMA's practitioners as safe as possible.

We make changes to our system often. We are looking for the most effective, easiest to recall and easiest to perform techniques possible. When we see something that we think may be easier, more effective, etc. we rep that technique until we are proficient at it. It's easy to try something once and like what you're doing already because, heck, you're good at the technique you've practiced for years. After we can explain exactly why what we are thinking of switching to is better we have one more step. We then have one of our small female instructors learn and perform the technique. If it isn't going to work for them, it doesn't get changed. WE can't change things if they don't work for everyone no matter their size, strength or athletic ability.

We change to keep people safe. We get griped at from time to time by USKMA instructors when we do make changes. It would be easy for us to just keep things the same. We might look smarter if we acted like we've had the answers all along. We're willing to catch flack from some of our instructors when changes are made because we take what we do seriously. For example, after teaching our long gun defenses for years we changed them to a much simpler, much better defense. I had LE instructors griping that they wish we'd taught them the new way years ago. I agreed…I wish I would have too! We taught something to many people that is now in the trash can. We found better and passed it along!

In the last six weeks alone we have changed one of our full nelson defenses (so that we don't fall with the attacker) and our slashing knife defense (so we wrap the attacking arm with our arms instead of grabbing a wrist). Over the years we have made a lot of changes to the curriculum that I was taught. In 1998 I was in one of the very first Krav Maga instructor trainings ever hosted in the U.S. I was taught by some very, very good instructors. I have spent time training with Grandmaster Yaron Lichtehnstein, one of only ten people the founder of Krav Maga, Imi Lichtenfeild, taught from beginner to black belt. I learned some great stuff. I would say that over the years we in the USKMA have changed 70% of what I was taught.

We have pretty much completely revamped what we taught for handgun, knife and long gun disarms. We simply found better, more reliable, easier and more effective techniques. Our "go to" handgun disarm is the cupping technique to get both hands on the weapon and deliver a groin kick. The one we replaced had the weapon controlled by one hand as the other hand punched the attacker. I always worried about a small female police officer trying to disarm a huge thug. I had no faith in that technique in that situation. We have changes all of the knife defenses from grabbing the wrist with our hand to wrapping the attacking arm with our arm. When a person attacks realistically (like a sewing machine needle) the grabbing the wrist defenses always worried me. Add a slick wrist (blood, etc.) and they became mighty hard to pull off. Our long gun had good techniques, just three totally different techniques. The front to the dead side, front to the live side and from behind were just as different from each other as could be…and they had a lot of steps. We basically now have one technique whether it's from the front of behind. Much easier to remember and a much stronger technique.

Some things I see being taught in other systems that make me wonder "why are they teaching that?" include:

- Techniques that only work if you perform them the second you are touched. I have seem a headlock defense, for example, taught that would only work if the person being attacked is standing straight up and reacts immediately. In reality, I didn't see the attacker coming. I am bent forward and knocked off balance and swung forward before I can possibly react. Better have a defense that works from there!

- Handgun defenses that go up. This always makes me want to tear my hair out! That gun is going off as you redirect it, the idiot's finger is on the trigger. Why would you purposely take the barrel of that gun across your brain bucket? I know of a police officer who turned a corner and immediately had a gun fired at his head. He reached out and redirected it offline the way he was taught and the bullet blew his front teeth out…and nothing else. If the defense that came out of him was to push the gun up he wouldn't have been around to tell the story.

- Knife defenses that require grabbing and manipulating the wrist. A realistic attack would prove this is virtually impossible. Attempt the defense with a realistic attack and your arms slathered with ky jelly (representing blood) and it becomes beyond virtually impossible. Here's what a realistic knife attack would look like:

- Techniques with several steps that must be followed. When I see these choreographed moves I think that the person performing them had better hope an attacker steps the same way, does the same things and reacts the same way that the practice partner does. If it's steps a through f and in the real world it derails at step c because the attacker did something different, the practitioner is in trouble.

- Techniques that think they know when the attacker will quit. I see instructors turning their back on an attacker after delivering a technique. Whether it was a punch to the throat, a kick to the groin, a "knockout blow" or a bone break they are teaching that it will end the attack. We have seen videos of people taking pipes across the head, several bullets mid torso, dozens of knife wounds…and they keep coming. Thinking you know what will stop an attacker is bad training. Go until they are done…and then still beat feet away from them!

- "Nonlethal" techniques. In other words, techniques for when you can't really kick someone in the groin, punch them in the face or the like. WTF? I have zero use for control techniques unless you are a bouncer, cop or in another job where you must control and not damage. To teach these to a female as self defense is reprehensible. If attacked in the real world there are no rules except to stay alive. The only way to do this is to swing for the fences with all the hatred and rage you can muster, attempting to deliver as much damage in as little time as humanly possible until you can get to safety.

Instructors, when people are coming to you for self defense training they are literally putting their lives in your hands. You had better be teaching the best stuff you can possibly find and not crap from a system just because it's your system! BE SAFE!

That Brutal Stuff

When I first started teaching Krav in 1998 very few people had heard of Krav Maga. When they had heard of it I almost always got the comment "Oh, that brutal stuff". My answer was always "I don't look at it as brutal, I look at it as effective. I didn't start the attack." Problem is, most people have no idea what real violence is or what real self defense needs to be. They learned from their martial arts instructor or from TV and movies…and believed it.

Whenever you have to use self defense you are already losing. You are trying to recover from stupidity or bad luck, as Rory Miller says. You have already taken some damage. Now, if the attacker is a pro and has done this before he knows what works. What works is a flurry attack that never lets you recover or hit back. We will be hit, stabbed or bludgeoned several times before we ever realize what is going on. We could be taking so much damage that we're out in just a few seconds without ever hitting back. So...if this works for the scumbag we had better study it and do it better. Again, as Rory Miller says, if the scumbag is going to use violence as a weapon we need to take that weapon, practice it and weald it better than they do.

So, in Krav Maga we don't just teach a block. We don't even just teach a block and simultaneous counter attack. We teach a block with a simultaneous punch into a kick to the groin into clinching and kneeing the idiot in the face and groin into dumping them onto the ground into stomping their Achilles and running away. To show less will get people hurt.

Something for men who teach self defense for women to think about. Guys, think of your nightmare attacker. The dude weighs 70 lbs. more than you, is way, way stronger than you, is way faster than you, is way more aggressive than you and has trained one hundred times more than you. His best punch to your head will for sure knock you out and will probably kill you. Your best punch to his head is just going to piss him off and he'll come at you even harder. Pretty damned scary, huh? This is the starting point for a woman learning self defense. Your nightmare attacker is her likely attacker. Why would you teach her to put her keys between her fingers, to blow a whistle, to carry something heavy in her purse to swing or to drop on the ground and get her feet between her and her attacker? Would any of that crap work for you? There is only one option that has any chance of saving your ass in that situation. That is to go forward with all the hatred and rage you can muster, become an animal. Spit, cuss, claw, bite and smash targets (eyes, throat, groin, knees, Achilles) over and over...always looking to escape. If that is the only thing that is gonna work for you that is what you better be teaching them.

Another quote from Rory Miller (the USKMA just had him in for a seminar so for the next several weeks you're going to hear from him a lot!), "the first person to go balls to the wall almost always wins." The scumbags know this and that is why they attack so brutally. We need to train the same way. Go at the attacker with such hatred and rage, swinging for the fences and being "brutal" that we win. Turn the strategy on them.

To teach self defense without ever studying what a realistic attack on the street looks like is crazy. The martial arts are about the only thing that you will find that works and works on answers without ever knowing what the question is. Just getting on youtube and watching a real knife attack would be enough for me to think "damn, that knife defense I have been working on would get me killed" and yet most of us don't do that. Almost everyone I see teaching self defense are actually teaching self defense techniques, not self defense. There is a difference.

I have had people leave my intros complaining that we are teaching over the top, that we are too brutal. This always saddens me as I know they have a pre conceived notion of what violence is, and that notion is wrong and can get them killed. If you are teaching self defense (and I've blogged this dozens of times) those coming to you are literally putting their lives in your hands. You had better be what violence is, had better not be teaching crap from a system just because it's your system. You are preparing people for what will be the most terrifying few minutes of their lives and the stakes are life and death. Lean, train smart and train the "brutal" stuff! BE SAFE!

Gym Techniques

I study a lot of other systems and go to a lot of self defense, safety and shooting seminars. I learn some good things but I also see a lot of gym techniques (or, in the shooting world, range techniques). By gym techniques I mean things that are taught that look good in the gym, make sense when explained, look devastating and way cool but, when you study real world violence & real world attacks and put some thought in to them….just wouldn't work on the streets. Too many systems, both self defense and shooting, add layers of complexity to techniques to justify their "secret formula" I do believe. Academically what they teach may well make sense but the problem is they have never asked the opinion of someone who has lived through a violent attack. This blog isn't to put anyone down but to challenge you to be a critical thinker and to study real world violence. Some of what I consider gym techniques:

- Most anything ground related that isn't taught as "you got knocked down…fight and get the hell back up". To patiently control until you can submit isn't a sound self defense strategy. In the gym it may look way devastating as you snap my elbow or tear my shoulder to shreds but on the street as you are doing that my friend is kicking you in the head, I am pulling my knife and slicing you or…I am slicing you as my friend kicks your head. So you snap my elbow, it didn't kill me. I now get up and beat the crap out of you with the three appendages I have left! Also, I need you to show me how awesome that stuff works out on the concrete…see how many times you want to knee drop as you take me down, stay on top of me as I buck and your knees smack the pavement, pull guard as your melon smacks the ground, etc.

- I have heard of entire weekend seminars on how to get out of restraints. I have been to home invasion seminars where they spend 1/3 of the day showing how to break zip ties that are put around your wrists. This seems like a good skill to have…until you think about it. I refuse to train this…I don't want it in my head that I will ever be restrained. I have decided (mind setting) that I will fight five guys with shotguns aimed at my head before I will be restrained. Once restrained my options go way down. I will only survive then if the scumbags decide to let me. I will have that say, not them. Those who teach this will say "Well, you could have been knocked out and woke up bound or they could have a gun to your kids head." Again, academically this makes sense. To me, they don't. About the being knocked out...the only reason I wake up from being knocked out is that the scumbags decided to not kill me. So right off the bat my scenario is based on being knocked out by good Bad Guys! When I do wake up so many things could have happened. They could be gone, they could have tied me hand and foot and done it right, I could be locked inside somewhere, I could be blah, blah, blah. You get the picture. I think training for a wishful thinking scenario is kinda a waste. Now, as far as the gun at my kid's head and I better comply, again, this decision has been made ahead of time. I will rush the gunman and pray that he points the gun at me as I approach. Even if I take a fatal wound I will take this piece of crap with me. If you study home invasions you know what the other alternative is. You will be forced to watch your family tortured, raped and probably killed. I ain't going out that way my friends.

- In the shooting world I have seen a system that teaches that if you pull the trigger and the gun doesn't fire to shuffle your feet moving back and forth as you clear the jam and put the weapon back in service. Again, this makes logical sense. As you are clearing that jam or reloading don't stand in one place as that makes it easier to hit you. I have had officers who have had to fire while being fired on tell me "Bull shit. If that gun don't go boom It could be it's empty, could be a jam and could be that it is broken and ain't gonna fire any more no matter what I do to it. Even if I fix that jam in a second and a half I am not staying in a three foot area shuffling back and forth as the idiot can fire 10 rounds at me in that time. If my weapon goes click I will sprint like I am on fire to the nearest cover and clear that jam as I am running. If and when I get it back to working order then I can get back on target and fire."

- Some training tools seem cool but make no sense to me. The one I am asked about often are those cool shock knives. They are training blades that have a battery and will give you a jolt if they touch you. When I am asked if we have these I always say "what purpose would they serve?" Yes, it will let me know when the knife touches me but what is that saying... that if I get touched by a knife I did the defense wrong? I say BS to that! It's a knife, you are going to get cut! If you are practicing knife defenses and not getting touched by the knife it is because the attacker isn't attacking you anywhere near realistically. "To fight on after you feel pain" may be a logical answer as well. Study the adrenaline dump and stress I would say. You aren't feeling anything while it's going on. The pain comes later when things are done.

- While we're on it, most any knife defense you have ever seen is a gym technique. If you can run that should be your first choice. If you can't run find something to smack the idiot with (a ball bat would work nicely). If those two things can't happen block as good as you can while punching the attacker's throat and kicking him in the groin. That's about as good as it gets if there is a knife involved. All those cool joint locks and ninja moves? When someone wants to show you one first slather baby oil or ky jelly on both of your arms from fingertip to elbow. When they cry "foul" point out to them that a knife is made to cut. If there is a knife involved there is blood involved. Blood is one slippery substance.

Any move that relies on squaring up and acquiring some distance is probably a gym technique. Violence just doesn't give you time to do that. It is on you fast and furious. Techniques with a lot of movement, big steps, pushing forward then pulling back, etc. are gym techniques. Learn to rely on having space and then you're screwed the one time you really are attacked and it's in a bus isle.

- Techniques that rely on being stronger or bigger than the opponent (I see a lot of these) are gym techniques...do you know in advance who is going to attack you? Any technique that you can't perform tired, stressed and confused is a gym technique. Put everything you learn under stress and exhaustion.

As I say in one of my lectures to new instructors "don't put your personal safety in the hands of some self appointed expert. Never let anything over ride your own experience and common sense. You are not children, think for yourselves!" BE SAFE!

What Would You Do If...

As a Krav Maga instructor I get asked quite often by students, family, general public, etc. "What would you do if...(jumped by ninjas, met multiple attackers with chain saws, were squared off with a UFC fighter, etc., etc., fill in the blank)?" My answer is almost always "I'd take out my big knife and slice them". After a weird look the person asking usually says "I don't carry a knife". This is where they get my smart aleck "You asked what I would do...not what you should do."

The person asking is usually looking for a specific technique to use against that chain saw, machete or bazooka. This is where I get to explain to them that we don't really teach techniques, we teach a self defense philosophy. That philosophy is to go now, go hard, go forward and swing for the fences. Techniques won't save your ass in a violent attack. Going forward with hatred and rage to destroy whatever is in front of you is what will save you. I've blogged many times that if you ask a cop who they would rather face; A) a very proficient martial artist or B) a crazy who wants to claw their face off and chew on their eyeballs I guarantee you that the cop will choose A every time.

So when asked what I would do if some crazy attack ever finds me the answers are easy.

- Why am I in a place where there are crazed ninjas in the first place? Don't go to stupid places with stupid people to do stupid things. Self defense is truly recovery from stupidity or bad luck.

- If I can I will run. Yep, 4th degree black belt in Taekwondo, National light wt. tkd sparring champion 33-40 y.o. division, 3rd degree black belt in Krav Maga, have taught self defense to thousands, author of three books on Krav Maga…and I would run. Nobody is unbeatable, there are always bigger, stronger and badder. More than one attacker is hard for anyone to handle. A person with just a little training with a weapon will beat an unarmed expert more often than not. Add all this up and the smartest thing to do in almost any violent situation is to beat feet!

- Find something to use as a weapon. I know many empty hand defenses to take a knife away from a knife wielding maniac. They are the best ever developed, tried and true, IDF approved and, yet, I'd take a ball bat and an attitude over any of them. Honestly, I'd take a ball bat and an attitude over a black belt in any system.

- If left with no other choice but to fight it is always "get rid of the danger and destroy the idiot." If choked get the attackers hands off my throat as I kick his groin, punch his throat, etc. If he is on top beating me its block and elbow his groin, punch his throat, bite, etc. If it's a knife block it and hit the idiot. If it's a handgun get it pointed so the bullet doesn't hit me and hit the idiot.

Notice how everything ends with "hit the idiot"? This is why half of every class in Krav Maga is spent on combatives. This is why we hit things often and hard in class. This is why I say that if a student drops out of a martial art after three months they really aren't very good but if they leave Krav Maga after only three months they have a decent chance of being able to defend themselves. We didn't have to do anything but show them how to hit hard and often and develop an attitude of "go hard, go forward" in them. This is the key to staying safe!

So when it's the crazy "what would you do if a guy had both an AK and a 12 gauge pointed at you?" It's easy to answer "Get the things pointed somewhere besides at me and beat the crap out of the idiot!" BE SAFE!

UFC

What the UFC taught me about self defense

Those that know me know that I am a big UFC fan. There was a time I wouldn't miss a fight (until they started putting them on every two weeks) nor would I miss an episode of the Ultimate Fighter (until the last two seasons when they decided 85% of the show should be extreme close up interviews with fighters who have nothing intelligent to say). I was teaching Krav Maga long before I got into MMA fights. What I have noticed over the years of watching fights confirms some things I knew...and surprised me with what I didn't know.

- Knockouts! We train to knock people out. If I am attempting a handgun defense, for example, and I can knock the idiot out...the defense is done! Watching the UFC has allowed me to see how friggin hard knocking someone out can be. There are a few guys with one punch knockout power, but they are rare. The best bet for a knockout is to stun the dude and then hit him over and over again until he goes down. Don't hesitate or let him recover. We teach this!! Go forward with rage and hatred and hit the scumbag over and over until you are safe!

- Knees. We train to clinch and knee a lot in Krav Maga. A knee to the head is a pretty significant strike. I was surprised to see so many dudes taking these to the noggin and keep fighting. This isn't for sure knockout that I always assumed it was.

- Ground. Those that are good at ground are sweet to watch. The thing that I notice mainly is how long it takes to submit. On the street if we factor in the guy's buddies running up to help we wouldn't have the time to submit. I still don't want to be on the ground...ever!

- Cardio. Exhaustion makes cowards of us all. The muscle heads usually lose! There are guys who look unbeatable in the first round that slow down later in the fight and get whooped. I have heard Israeli instructors state that if your Krav Maga gym has cardio classes it isn't a real Krav Maga gym. This is a stupid statement! If you can fight hard for a longer period of time you are safer. I do not see how this can be argued!

- Fear. You can see it in some of the fighters. They usually talk big and say things like "He'll have to kill me before I stop", etc., etc., blah, blah. They then get in the ring and freeze before purposely giving up their back so they can tap. I tell my students to think only of going forward with rage and swing for the fences. Don't look at how mean or big the dude is, just look at targets.

- You have to be well rounded. It took the UFC for fighters to realize this. The first events were one style against another. When the Gracie's won they all decided they had better learn ground. Imi was preaching this in the 40's and 50's. A man ahead of his time.

- Everyone can be whooped. After the baddest man on the planet, the unbeatable Brock Lesner lost twice in a row he retired. Anyone can be beat. Very few fighters in the UFC are undefeated. Again, if attacked by a big, mean looking dude don't see the dude, see only targets.

- Cheat! No matter how big and strong the fighter is he flops on the ground like he's dying if he gets kicked in the groin or has an eye poked. There is a system being taught that says to never kick to the groin, it is a wasted strike. Say what? All I have to do is watch a fight… those groin shots look pretty effective. The things that are against the rules in MMA fighting are exactly what we want to do on the street. They are against the rules because they do damage and end fights too quickly. Doing damage and ending fights quickly is what we're all about!!

The Knockout "Game"

I have been asked several times lately about the "knockout game" that is in the news and all over social media. First off, let's not follow the news media's lead and call it a game! It's only a game to the thug pieces of s#$t that are "playing" it. If you haven't heard about this, it is basically a group of people (generally teens, generally racially motivated) that think its fun to randomly attack and knock out an unsuspecting victim while they video the attack. People are asking me what to do like it's a new phenomenon. Random violent attacks are pretty much what we've been training people to defend against since Krav Maga was founded…this crap happens all the time.

What should we do about it? Well, first and foremost have a plan. It's kinda nice that it is all over social media because people are aware of it, talking about it and thinking about it. These same people, before this hit the news, never thought about a random violent idiot picking them out. Again, this didn't just start happening! Now that we are thinking about it we can mind set!

My advice about avoiding the "knockout game" is the same advice I have given in Krav Maga classes for fifteen years! First and foremost, don't go to stupid places with stupid people to do stupid things! I won't come across a gang attacking people because I live in the country…I'm lucky to see four people in a day! Now I realize we all aren't that blessed and we must live and work in cities but is there ever a reason to go to a bad part of town? If your job doesn't make you go there why go there to shop, eat or anything else? Avoiding areas where this is happening (mainly downtown in big cities) cuts your odds of being attacked way, way down.

Second, if a stranger is going to pass you, keep an eye on him/her and have a plan about what you will do if they do lunge at you. Even more relevant would be if a group of strangers are going to pass you, keep an eye on them and have a plan about what you will do if they lunge at you! I have heard several police officers quote the saying "Be polite and professional with every person you come across…and have a plan to kill them." This is being safe. Yes, be a good person but always have a plan to beat someone down if they do turn on you. There isn't a person I walk past that I don't look at out of the corner of my eye looking to see if they might burst my way. I am planning on blocking an attack and simultaneously punching them in the throat or kicking them in the jimmies! Is this paranoid? It sounds like there are a bunch of hurting folks across the nation that wish they had been a bit more paranoid.

Have a plan but have a realistic plan. To think that you will draw a handgun or knife misses the point of what a sucker punch is. A sucker punch is a punch you don't' see!! You don't have time for this! Your flinch reaction must be (if you see it at the last second or feel someone closing on you) to tuck your chin. This is all you are going to get out of you but to take a punch on the top of the head/forehead is way better than taking one in the soft part of your face. Now, go forward and make them pay!! If you have a bit more warning block that punch and attack… and then access a weapon.

Notice that I said I watch everyone I go by? This would mean not texting or otherwise farting with a smart phone as you go down the street. Ya think the scumbags might be looking for the oblivious person who is absorbed in something else and not paying attention? I'd bet they are. Be alert at all times.

If you have a gut feeling that something is amiss there is no reason not to make a scene yelling your head off or to start beating feet in the opposite direction. If three or four guys are approaching you and start to spread as if they are wanting to all get to you at different angles, alarm bells should be going off in your head. Don't wait to see if those feelings you had were right…react right away! If you've told someone to not approach you and they keep coming… that someone needs hit hard. Hitting first is smart…don't wait. Why would someone not stop when you have told them to? Because they have good intentions?

My personal "mind setting" plans? If a group of teens are approaching me and I feel there's something amiss I will cross the street or otherwise change the path I was headed in. If they then change directions it's on. I will run if I have the distance and time. If they are a bit closer and I think running won't save me I plan on putting my back against the wall, drawing the big knife I carry and act like I'm cleaning my finger nails…all the while making eye contact so they know that I know what's going on. If its last second and I have no time for either of these things, and I feel there is no other recourse, I will start the knockout game. I will take some people out and get out of Dodge! I may not win that but its last resort…and I will take as many with me as I can! BE SAFE!

Swing For The Fences!

"If it has limitations it isn't self defense"
—M. Slane

I see a lot of "self defense" systems that come from the "non-lethal" angle. They put limitations on what their practitioners can do. This always makes me shake my head. Several of these systems claim their goal is to "restrain or stop an attack while causing minimal injury to the attacker". I also see systems that use adjuncts such as sticks, canes, leather straps, etc. to "strike non-lethal targets to make the attacker back off". My thought is that if you are a bouncer, school teacher, cop or the like this may be what you need to learn for your job. These people are learning a system that make them personally not as safe, they are trading keeping themselves safe for what they need to know for their job. IF you don't have to learn such a system for your job why in the world would you learn it at all?

Quite a few martial arts take this same approach. They have a "never strike first" or a "never do more harm than necessary" warriors code of ethics. Even BJJ (which I respect immensely) has the philosophy of "patiently contain until you can submit" while allowing no punches to the throat, eye gouges or groin strikes. None of this makes sense to me! To put limitations on self defense is to put people in danger! The scumbags don't have these codes or philosophies, aren't worried about being non-lethal or restraining. To teach our students such things puts them behind the eight ball. The bad guys are using violence as a weapon. We must take this weapon of violence, perfect it and weald it better than they do!

Most systems and arts can teach whatever bullshit they want, it will never be tested in the real world. Heaven help their students if it ever is. I don't know how instructors that teach these things could sleep at night if one of their students ever got hurt bad with the crap they are taught. As I tell my instructors "when someone comes to you for self defense they are literally putting their lives in your hands." To show a small female one of these systems where they are taught to restrain and not do "too much damage" is setting them up to be badly hurt or killed. When the attacker is bigger and stronger than you, when there are more than one attackers, when you are ambushed, etc. the only thing that has even a little bit of a chance of getting you out alive is to fight like a cornered animal with all the rage, aggression and hatred you can muster. You must become a crazy person thinking only of doing the maximum amount of damage you possibly can and then to get away. You must gouge eyes, slam into throats and groins, bust knees and put people down! To teach anything else is to set people up for failure.

My favorite quote from Rory Miller's books is "Listening to most martial artists talk about real world violence is like listening to ten year olds talk about sex". When I do instructor training during one of my lectures I ask "who is teaching self defense?" Most raise their hand. I then ask them who has studied violence, who has studied how the scumbags think and attack? Who has read Rory Miller's Meditations on Violence & Facing Violence? Who has read Col. Grossman's On Combat & On Killing? Who has read DeBecker's Gift of Fear or SGT Strong's Strong on Defense? I usually see zero hands raised at this point. I then tell them "If you haven't studied violence, studied how the scumbags attack, know what a realistic attack is, know what stops people or know what group strategies they use, how the hell can you think you are teaching self defense?" BE SAFE!!

Train For What You Will See

I have blogged on this subject several times. It amazes me that self defense arts and systems teach techniques that look cool but have never been put under stress, exhaustion, the adrenaline dump, etc. If we are ever violently attacked I can guarantee that there will be plenty of each of those. I see this often with handgun and knife defenses. The attacker stands there like a statue in a warm and dry gym and the practitioner practices a technique. On the street there is blood that makes the weapon slippery, the weapon is moving constantly, the attack was a surprise, the attacker is hitting, kicking and cussing us, etc. IF we had not practiced for any of those things we will be lost. If we train that way we will have a "been there, done that" feeling and our training will come out of us.

The following paragraph is from a blog by the USKMA's co-lead instructor, Brannon Hicks:

> "If I want to win BJJ tournaments, I should go to a BJJ school. If I want to win Muay Thai boxing matches, I should train at a Muay Thai gym. While my training at both of those gyms might be outstanding and produce the result I sought out, neither would adequately prepare me for the street. I train mixed martial artists as well, and Krav Maga is not what I use to prepare them for the cage; it simply would not produce the desired result. So, if I am a LEO who will have to fight a subject into handcuffs, or perhaps face multiple attackers with and without weapons in a violent encounter where I don't win titles but I do win my survival, why would I only train in systems designed to win tournaments or sporting events? It is clear to me that when I train, the way that I train must prepare me to win the types of situations I may face."

I couldn't have put it better. If we are training for real violence on the street it makes no sense to practice a sport centered art or system. I get this sometimes with the training I do for higher level Krav Maga students. They sometimes seem to think rank is more important than actually having performed under actual violent attacks. For example, I can have someone teach Muay Thai who has been in the art for several years. They are proficient and know the techniques but haven't sparred much. The other choice is someone who has been in the art only half of the time as the "master" but has been in dozens of fights. I'll take the guy who has done it under stress and exhaustion over the master any day. I am not worrying about pretty techniques, I am worried about survival. Another example, I have a choice of who I am going to learn ground fighting from. The first choice is a BJJ master who is very proficient and a good instructor. My other choice is a police officer who has no real rank in BJJ but who is on the ground every month or so fighting a thug who is trying to kill him (or at least do great bodily harm). I want to learn from the guy who's actually fought for his life, who has done it under stress and with great exhaustion. Theory and proficiency are great but I'll take the guy who has done it under extreme exhaustion and stress in real violent encounters every time!

The point is rank is nice but if it's just proficiency of techniques that have never been put under stress and exhaustion how do I know it'll save my butt when my butt needs saved? I go with the doers and could care less who has what rank and for how long.

BJJ and Self Defense

"However beautiful the strategy, one should occasionally look at the results."
—Winston Churchill

Oh, let the fun begin. I run this post once a year...it gets more comments than any other blog I have written. Let me start out, as usual, by saying that I absolutely respect BJJ. BJJ is like chess on the mat, the practitioners have to be very smart and in awesome shape. Most of the instructors at the Krav gyms I owned did BJJ with my blessing. I had a BJJ black belt teaching BJJ classes at my gyms. I believe that we have to be well rounded and know what the heck we are doing on the ground. My son takes BJJ at a gym and I love what he is learning! I could have him in any discipline but I chose BJJ for him. There is nothing better for a school yard, one on one fight.

What slays me are the people advertising BJJ as the ultimate in self defense. I just ran across a web site for a BJJ gym that said "Krav Maga will get you killed". They actually said that statistically most fights are one on one bar room type fights with no weapon involved so it is a waste of time to train for anything but this type of one on one fighting. Even if this is a true statistical statement do we ignore any other type of attack because it is in the minority? Weapons certainly exist, run a daily google search for knife attacks or shootings across the country. Your in box will be full! People do get attacked by multiple attackers, people do get shot or stabbed and sexual assaults do happen. Because 50,000 of 80,000 daily attacks in the U.S. don't involve a weapon or multi attackers that's good enough reason not to train for weapons and multi attackers? What kind of logic is that…oh yeah, it's the "I make money off of what I teach" kind of logic.

BJJ is an awesome sport but to train it alone for self defense absolutely ignores real world violence. It is absolutely betting the practitioner's life on the fact that there will only be one attacker and there won't be a blade involved. BJJ's philosophy is to patiently control an opponent until they can be submitted. In the real world every scumbag has a scumbag friend nearby. We should always be looking to end things as quickly as possible and to get the heck out of there. I have a friend who told me about a buddy of his that went to a "BJJ for the street" gym. He got into an altercation in a bar and pulled guard on his attacker like he was taught. The guy drew a knife and stabbed him seven times. Another friend told me of a BJJ black belt who wrapped a guy up in a bar in just a few seconds, looked awesome doing it…right up until the guy's buddy kicked the black belt in the face, broke his jaw and knocked him out. If you are on the ground tied up with someone you are absolutely making the assumption that he doesn't have a knife and doesn't have a buddy. These are not assumptions that will keep you safe.

From a thread on our old website by my friend Aaron Jannetti; "If you understand the nature of violence, and how easy it is to harm someone, you will quickly understand that two places you don't want to be are on the ground or wrapped up with someone."

There are some very impressive techniques which would absolutely get you f'd up with a violent individual in an icy parking lot.

Don't believe me, fine. Here is the experiment. Find someone who you think can kick your ass with their grappling. Tell them to grab you up. Your only job is to see how many times you can stick your fingers on their eye brow ridge or grab the inside of their leg next to their testicles. Every time you can touch their eyebrow is a time you could have gotten a finger in to their orbital socket. Every time you touch their leg is a ripped sack or torn off junk. You will quickly find the limitations of someone trying to hold you down on the floor.

Second experiment, grappler vs edged weapon. Take a magic marker, put it in your pocket. Have your ass whupping grappler put the ju-ju on you. Your only task is to get to the marker, and touch them with it. Their job is to shut you down. Much learning will take place."

Have you ever tried BJJ on concrete or blacktop? I've had friends who have and they inform me that there is no good position. Being on the bottom gets you ground into hamburger. Knees and elbows get torn to shreds when in side-control. The mount sounds good until the opponent starts bucking and your knees slam over and over into the pavement.

That magic mount is such a strong position in the MMA ring. In the real world the dude on the bottom puts you in a big bear hug until his buddy can get over to ya and kick your head off. I had a friend who was a bouncer at a bar years ago. One night he took down a thug and broke his arm at the elbow with an armbar because the thug kept fighting. After breaking the thug's arm he let loose, started to sit up and got cold cocked by the guy's other fist. Broken bones and joints suck, but they aren't an end all. Self defense ain't over til you are safe and out of there.

I hate seeing women's self defense instructors teach women to hit the ground. Women should be fighting with one goal and one goal only...to escape. Being wrapped up with the scumbag on the ground makes escape harder. Bad plan in my opinion. Worse yet is all of the law enforcement training I see being done with BJJ alone. Do you know why BJJ practitioners pin their opponents face up? To give the opponent a better chance of escaping. Law enforcement officers should definitely be putting suspects on their face, worrying about weapons and expecting a scumbag's buddy to jump in. Trying to patiently control until you can submit isn't smart in that context.

We just had training at our affiliate weekend on a bus. Multiple attackers, blades, handguns, etc. We had some BJJ guys in the training. How much of their BJJ do you think worked in that situation? The only way anyone got on the ground was to fall just right in the aisle. Aisles are pretty tight, there was no room to move once there. They ended up just wailing on the attacker with fists, biting and head butting because that's all they could do.

Again, I am not bad mouthing BJJ at all. I am bad mouthing those who are telling students that BJJ is all the self defense they need for real world violence. I believe BJJ is a great PART of a total self defense system. Now, instead of name calling and talking about my dear mama in the comment section how about we have a discussion we can all learn from where the above points are refuted?

12

In Closing

*"When things look bad and it looks like you're not gonna make it…
then you gotta get mean. I mean plumb mad dog mean cuz if you lose
your head and you give up then you neither live nor win. That's just
the way it is."*
—The Outlaw Josey Wales

Instructors, first off make sure what you show your students is the most street proven, scientific and effective stuff out there. Don't show crap from a system just because it's your system. Don't teach what is hot at the moment. An example of this is when Brazilian Jiu Jitsu became very popular a lot of Law Enforcement training started to be BJJ. Common sense tells us that we don't want to be on the ground with a criminal. A knife or a second attacker makes the ground a dangerous place to be. Another interesting thing about BJJ is that they pin people face up. This is a rule that is in BJJ to give the person being pinned a better chance, to make the matches more even. Why would we in law enforcement want to do that? We should be pinning the suspect face down!

If you have techniques for any of the situations in this book that you like better please, by all means, stick with what you think works best. We only ask that you be able to articulate why what you are doing is better. Don't think something is better because that is what you have practiced more or have taught for years but only think it's a better technique because you can verbalize exactly why it is easier, more effective and will keep you and those you teach safer. Give Krav Maga an honest try and I believe that it will keep you, and those you train, safer.

The main thing to remember as instructors is that to teach only techniques is a SIN! To save a life (your own or someone else's) the technique is maybe 40% of what the officer needs. How

 215

many dash cam videos have you seen where the officer in the fight is doing anything that even remotely resembles his/her training? I would guess not very often. It is almost as if we survive in spite of our training, not because of it. Much more important than the techniques that are taught is the attitude and philosophy that is being taught. The attitude must be "I am going home today no matter what." We must teach aggression, a fighting "never say die" spirit and we put all training into realistic scenarios. The drills in this book must be done to get proper training. We cannot just teach techniques as an end all but must practice the techniques under stress, while exhausted and under realistic circumstances. If we train a handgun disarm, for example, always with the partner standing like a statue with the handgun pointed at us it is an entirely different feeling on the street when the attacker is punching us with the gun, slapping us, cussing and screaming. If we had never had an attacker come at us like this we haven't trained for it, we won't have a plan and it will not come out of us. If we train properly we will have the "been there, done that" feeling that we need to stay safe. Another example is with our knife defenses. If we've only practiced these static in a gym it will be a completely different feeling when the attacker is slashing and moving and when there is blood involved. If there is a knife involved there will be blood spilled...and blood is one slippery substance. Have most of us ever trained for this? Train knife defenses with KY jelly slathered all over your arms. Now when there is blood in the real world you are ready for it....things work differently when we attempt our defenses on slippery appendages.

Train hard, train putting everything you do under stress and exhaustion, train often and...BE SAFE!

Self Defense Education

"A nation that will insist on drawing a broad line of demarcation between the fighting man and the thinking man will have its fighting done by fools and its thinking done by cowards."
—Sir William Francis Butler

I tell those going through the USKMA's instructor training that if they teach self defense to others and don't read these books listed below it is like asking someone to learn from a history professor who has never read a history book! Sometimes I hear "I don't like to read." My thought on that is that I don't like to exercise but I do it because it's good for me! I want USKMA instructors to be educated, not just parroting what others told them. When students come to us for self defense they are literally putting their lives in our hands. We should know what real violence is, know what stress, the adrenaline dump and exhaustion do to us, know what kept people alive who have actually been there, etc., etc. The reading list I recommend to anyone teaching self defense (in order of my recommendation):

- Meditations On Violence by SGT Rory Miller. An amazing book. Learn about real world violence from a guy who's seen a bunch of it.

- Facing Violence by SGT Rory Miller. Goes over everything you could want to know about having to face real world violence. Talks about how to spot potential conflict, body language to look for to tell you an attack is coming, what stress and adreniline will do to you, how you will feel afterwards, what the police will want to hear and what they will do, what the court system will do to you, etc., etc. A must read!

- Strong On Defense by SGT Samford Strong. A tough read but a must read for those teaching self defense. Several interviews with people who have survived crimes.

- Conflict Communication by SGT Rory Miller. See the monkey dance and head it off.

- The Gift of Fear by Gavin DeBecker. Another must read. Will have you listening more to those voices in your head.

- On Killing and On Combat by Lt. Col. Dave Grossman. Shows us what BS the movies have told us about killing and violence. Studies how stress, adrenaline, etc. will affect us.

- Blink by Malcom Gladwell. Ever just had a feeling about something? This book explains why and will have you listening to those feelings from now on!

- The Book Of Five Rings by Miyomato Musashi. There really is nothing new. What some self defense gurus are saying is theirs and new was done thousands of years ago!

- In the Name of Self Defense by Marc MacYoung. Marc's been writing books for decades... you can't go wrong with any of them!

- Deep Survival by Laurence Gonzales. Why do some survive an incident while others perish during the same incident? Cool book.

- The Survivor's Club by Ben Sherwood. Very similar to the book above.

- Sharpening The Warrior's Edge by Bruce Siddle. Scientifically explains how we should be training for life and death situations.

- Training at the Speed of Life by Kenneth Murray. Similar to the above book.

- Combat Focus Shooting by Rob Pincus. Takes the no BS approach to shooting that Krav Maga does with self defense.

- Inside the Criminal Mind by Stanton Samenow. A bit dry but you'll understand the scumbags better...and quit feeling sorry for their poor childhoods.

- The Truth About Self Protection by Massad Ayoob. An expert in the field.

- Mark Slane has a couple of books that are definitely recommended by...Mark Slane. Be Safe, Self Defense For Women in the Real World, American Krav Maga and Krav Maga for Law Enforcement. Available on Amazon or on uskma.com.

- Probably should have been at the top of the list but the Bible. Cool stories of dudes taking on long odds and kicking butt. Even one about a guy who took the jaw bone of an ass and killed 1,000 heathens!

Here are my all-time favorite self defense quotes:

"You must train in chaos in order to thrive in chaos"
—Hock Hochheim

"Violence of motion trumps technique"
—Deputy US Marshall J. Jones

"However beautiful the strategy, you should occasionally look at the results."
—Winston Churchill

"If you want to control variables, hit first. If you don't or aren't able to hit first, you better know how to fight"
—R. Hoover

"If it has limitations it isn't self defense!"
—M. Slane

"The only defense against violent, evil people are good people who are more skilled at violence."
—SGT Rory Miller

"Surviving violent encounters is a matter of mastering fundamentals, being meaner than a junkyard dog and getting lucky."
—SGT Brannon Hicks

"Krav Maga is my support system for when my sucker punch didn't work."
—R. Hoover

"Self defense is recovery from stupidity or bad luck."
—SGT Miller

"Self defense is a short list of techniques that may get you out alive when you're already screwed"
—SGT Miller

"Instructors, when someone is coming to you to learn self defense they are literally putting their lives in your hands!"
—M. Slane

"When self defense becomes complicated, it is no longer self defense."
—R. Hoover

"Your instructor, system, art and cool techniques won't save you. Going forward, going hard, going now and going off with all the hatred and rage you can muster will."
—M. Slane

"When any person, idea, technique, school, piece of gear, team or tactic is put on a pedestal, we risk stopping progress."
—Rob Pincus

"Don't hit at all if it is honorably possible to avoid hitting; but never hit soft."
—Teddy Roosevelt

"Danger, if met head on, can be nearly halved"
—W. Churchill

"If I learn 1,000 techniques with my luck I'll go out on the street and be attacked by number 1,001."
—J. Whitman

"Every asshole has an asshole buddy nearby."
—M. Slane

"They'll eventually let ya out of prison, you're in the casket for good."
—M. Slane

"After initial contact all plans go to hell"
—Patton

"The wicked flee when no man pursues but the righteous are bold as a lion."
—Proverbs 28:1

"No matter how enmeshed a commander becomes in his plans, it is occasionally necessary to consider the enemy"
—W. Churchill

"You do not get to pick what kind of bad things will happen to you."
—SGT Miller

"We don't call it knife defenses, we call it Knife survival."
—SGT MJR Nir Maman

"Everybody's got a plan until they get smacked in the face"
—M. Tyson

"If ya ain't cheating, ya ain't trying"
—Various sources

"Home intruders are terrorists without a political agenda."
—SGT Sanford Strong

"If you're in a fair fight your tactics suck!"
—Various

"Krav Maga, so that one may walk in peace."
—Imi Lichtenfeld

"Self defense is the 'flinch' reaction to go from overwhelmed, terrified and uncomprehending to moving forward with rage and aggression to do the maximum amount of damage in the minimum amount of time."
—M. Slane

"Ask any police officer whom they would rather face…1) a very proficient martial artist or 2) a crazy who wants to claw their face and chew on their eyes. They take the martial artist every time".
—SGT Miller–paraphrased

"If the scumbags are going to use violence as a weapon we must perfect this weapon of violence and wield it better than they do".
—SGT Miller

"I don't have takedown defense? My fist is my takedown D!"
—S. Slane – 5 y.o.

"When it comes time, sheep bleat, but the knife falls anyway. Do something to survive."
—Rocky Warren

"First class training is the best form of welfare for the troops...the more you sweat in training, the less you bleed in battle."
—Irwin Rommel

"Give me a ball bat and an attitude over a black belt in any system."
—M. Slane

"When things look bad and it looks like you're not gonna make it... then you gotta get mean. I mean plumb mad dog mean cuz if you lose your head and you give up then you neither live nor win. That's just the way it is."
—The Outlaw Josey Wales

"You are not paranoid for thinking that there are people out there who may try to kill you if there are indeed people out there who may try to kill you."
—SGT S. Strong

"When a wolf bites a sheep the sheep bleats, rolls over and die. When a wolf bites a sheepdog the sheepdog gets pissed off and bites back."
—Col. Grossman

"If you aren't putting everything you teach under stress and exhaustion you are teaching self defense techniques, not self defense. There is a big difference."
—M. Slane

"You go for a man hard enough and fast enough, he don't have time to think about how many's with him; he thinks about himself, and how he might get clear of that wrath that's about to set down on him."
—Rooster Cogburn

"In any moment of decision, the best thing you can do is the right thing, the next best thing is the wrong thing, and the worst thing you can do is nothing."
—Theodore Roosevelt

"Don't be there in the first place because that means you messed up bad. Now it's all how bad you want to survive!"
—Tim Fisher

"To be prepared for war is one of the most effectual means of preserving peace."
—G. Washington

"Violence should, if justified, be used with neither hesitation nor regret."
—Cowan

"Have no thought but that of cutting your enemy down and it will express itself through you."
—Miyomato Musashi – book of five rings

"Preventing a violent encounter is much better than surviving a violent encounter." SGT
—Brannon Hicks

"We cannot be prepared for something we don't believe can happen."
—N. Mandela

"Be peaceful, be courteous, obey the law, respect everyone; but if someone puts his hand on you, send him to the cemetery."
—Malcolm X

"If there are no police agencies or military units using the same techniques and tactics today that they did even forty years ago, why would I think a centuries old martial art is cutting edge self defense?"
—M. Slane

"It's hard to beat a person who never gives up."
—Babe Ruth

"I won't be wronged. I won't be insulted. I won't be laid a-hand on. I don't do these things to other people, and I require the same from them."
—John Wayne in The Shootist

"When your goal is to end a situation it's amazing how many more options you have than when your goal is to 'win.'"
—Marc MacYoung

"If violent crime is to be curbed, it is only the intended victim who can do it. The felon does not fear the police, and he fears neither judge nor jury. Therefore, what he must be taught to fear is his victim."
—Lt. Col. Jeff Cooper

More from SGT Rory Miller:

"If talking is going to get you killed, it's time to stop talking."

"We are all immortal on every day but one."

"Listening to the average martial artists talk about real world violence is like listening to ten year olds talk about sex."

"knowing something is almost useless under stress, but understanding is often helpful."

"To manage fear you only need to believe you can do things. To manage danger you must be able to do things."

"No intelligent man has ever lost a fight to someone who said 'I'm gonna kick your ass'."

"It is much easier and safer to scare someone into submission than to beat them into submission."

"You fight like you train is only true if you train dumb, clumsy, blind and deaf."

"Use the environment. The difference between a hazard and a gift is who sees it first."

Further Training

Keep an eye on USKMA.com and like the United States Krav Maga Associations Facebook page to see upcoming seminars and trainings. If you would like to host a seminar contact us at Info@USKMA.com.

Affiliate locations:

Sidekicks Family Martial Arts Centers
16313 FishHawk Blvd.
Lithia, Florida

Florida Martial Arts & Fitness Center
5494 SW 50th Ct.
Ocala, Florida 34470

Florida Fit Factory
13790 Treeline Ave. South #4
Ft. Myers, Florida 33913

St. John's Krav Maga and Crossfit
1515 County Road 210
St. John's, Florida 32259

Dynamic Krav Maga
298 Dunlop Blvd. Bldg. 300
Huntsville, Alabama 35824

Elite Self Defense Systems
5695 Strathmoor Dr. Unit 2
Rockford, IL

Williams Karate Studio
West Liberty, KY

Caudill Krav Maga
3436 U.S. 421
Harlan Kentucky 40831

Elite Martial Arts & Fitness
124 Mini Mall Dr.
Brea, Kentucky 40403

Elite Martial Arts & Fitness–Richmond
5006 Atwood Dr. Ste 5
Richmond, Kentucky 40475

Shreveport Krav Maga
9101 Industrial Rd
Shreveport, Louisiana 71129

Marshall Tae Kwon Do Academy
1304A Five Notch Rd.
Marshall, Texas 75672

Powerkix Martial Arts
263 Garrisonville Rd. Ste 111A
Stafford, Virginia 22554

Longview Krav Maga
2901 N. Eastman Rd.
Longview, Texas 75605

Gilmer Krav Maga
902 US 271 N
Gilmer, Texas 75644

East Texas Martial Arts
4614 DC Drive Ste 1F
Tyler, Texas 75701

Buckeye Crossfit
6461 N Hamilton Rd.
Columbus, Ohio 43081

Delaware Fit Factory
171 S. Sandusky
Delaware, Ohio 43015

Reaction Krav Maga
4435 Boardman-Canfield Rd.
Canfield, Ohio 44406

McKinney Krav Maga
5101 McKinney Ranch Pkwy. Ste 120
McKinney, Texas 75070

Executive Self-Defense and Fitness Factory
115 Aero Country Rd
McKinney, Texas 75071

ATA Elite Martial Arts
540 North Grandstaff
Auburn, Indiana 46706

Martial Arts Advantage
830 S. Elm Pl.
Broken Arrow, Oklahoma 74012

Jenks Martial Arts Academy
708 W. Main
St. Jenks, Oklahoma 74037

Relentless Krav Maga and Fitness
45 N. Main Street
Manteno, Illinois 60950

Allen Park Martial Arts Center
7318 Park Ave.
Allen Park, Michigan 48101

New Breed Krav Maga
10004 S. 76th Ave. Unit N D
Bridgeview, Illinois 60467

DuPage Krav Maga
22W580 Poss St.
Glen Ellyn, Illinois 60137

CrossFit No Regrets
20 Main St.
North Reading, Massachusetts 01864

Dragon Within Martial Arts
11 Franklin St.
Salem, Massachusetts 01970

Empower Martial Arts
Unit 1 & 2 Puzzle Lane
Newton, New Hampshire 03858

Aurora Krav Maga
15428 E. Hampden Ave.
Aurora, Colorado 80013

Warrior Combat and Fitness
32214 Ellingwood Trail Ste 106/107
Evergreen, Colorado 80439

Roaring Fork Krav Maga
402 Park Ave.
Basalt, Colorado 81621

Ultima Self-Defense and Fitness East
7649 East Speedway Blvd.
Tucson, Arizona 85629

Ultima Self-Defense and Fitness Northwest
6781 Thornydale Rd.
Tucson, Arizona 85701

Champion Martial Arts
7900 W. Tropical Pkwy. Ste 110
Las Vegas, Nevada 89149

CrossFit Modesto
4213 McHenry Ave.
Modesto, California 95356

Alaska Krav Maga
1896 Marika Rd.
Fairbanks, Alaska

47454529R00136

Made in the USA
Charleston, SC
09 October 2015